THE UNITED NATIONS IN A CHANGING WORLD

THE MELLAND SCHILL LECTURES
*delivered at the University of Manchester
and published by the University Press*

The Law of International Institutions in Europe
by A. H. Robertson, B.C.L., S.J.D., 1961

The Role of International Law in the Elimination of War
by Professor Quincy Wright, 1961

The Acquisition of Territory in International Law
by Professor R. Y. Jennings, 1962

The Sources and Evidences of International Law
by Clive Parry, LL.D., 1965

Rights in Air Space
by D. H. N. Johnson, M.A., LL.B., 1965

International Law and the Practitioner
by Sir Francis A. Vallat, K.C.M.G., Q.C., 1966

The Law of the Sea
by D. W. Bowett, M.A., LL.B., Ph.D., 1967

International Law and the Uses of Outer Space
by J. E. S. Fawcett, M.A., 1968

Modern Diplomatic Law
by M. Hardy, M.A., LL.M., 1968

The United Nations in a Changing World
by J. A. C. Gutteridge, M.A., 1969

OTHER BOOKS ON INTERNATIONAL LAW

Self-defence in International Law
by D. W. Bowett, M.A., LL.B., Ph.D.

Human Rights in Europe
by A. H. Robertson, B.C.L., S.J.D.

The Legal Problems of Foreign Investment in Developing Countries
by E. I. Nwogugu, LL.B., Ph.D.

Human Rights in National and International Law
edited by A. H. Robertson, B.C.L., S.J.D.

Legal Aspects of Foreign Investment in the European Economic Community
by W. H. Balekjian, Dr. rer. pol., Dr. Jur., Ph.D.

The Settlement of Boundary Disputes in International Law
by A. O. Cukwurah, B.C.L., LL.B., Ph.D.

*East European Rules on the Validity of International Commercial
Arbitration Agreements*
by L. Kos-Rabcewicz-Zubkowski, LL.D.
[Out of print: *The United Nations: the first ten years*]

THE UNITED NATIONS IN A CHANGING WORLD

by

J. A. C. GUTTERIDGE

M.A. (Oxon.)

MANCHESTER UNIVERSITY PRESS
U.S.A.: OCEANA PUBLICATIONS INC.

© 1969 Manchester University Press

Published by the University of Manchester at
THE UNIVERSITY PRESS
316–324 Oxford Road, Manchester M13 9NR
UK standard book number: 7190 0400 4

U.S.A.

OCEANA PUBLICATIONS INC.
75 Main Street, Dobbs Ferry, N.Y. 10522
Library of Congress catalog card number: 71 102444

distributed in India by
N. M. TRIPATHI (PRIVATE) LIMITED
Princess Street, Bombay 2

Printed in Great Britain by Butler & Tanner Ltd., Frome and London

CONTENTS

		Page
FOREWORD by Professor B. A. Wortley		vii
I THE CHARTER AS A LIVING DOCUMENT		1
II THE MAINTENANCE OF INTERNATIONAL PEACE AND SECURITY		
(1) UNITING FOR PEACE		14
The absence of 'special agreements' under article 43		18
The lack of unanimity of the permanent members of the Security Council		18
The Uniting for Peace resolution		19
III THE MAINTENANCE OF INTERNATIONAL PEACE AND SECURITY		
(2) PEACE-KEEPING OPERATIONS		28
The 'police action' in Korea		29
The United Nations Emergency Force		31
The United Nations Force in the Congo		33
The legal basis for the United Nations forces in the Middle East and the Congo		36
The United Nations forces in Cyprus		40
The United Nations Temporary Executive Authority		42
The Special Committee on Peace-keeping		43
The continuing need for United Nations peace-keeping forces		44
IV NON-SELF-GOVERNING TERRITORIES		48
The origin of chapter XI of the charter		48
Independence as an objective		49
Self-determination		51
The implementation of chapter XI of the charter		53
Factors indicating the attainment of independence or self-government		55
Resolution 1541 (XV)		58

v

186707

Resolution 1514 (XV)   60

The situation with regard to the implementation of the
declaration   63

Recent views on the scope of the principle of self-
determination   66

V SOME RECENT DEVELOPMENTS IN THE FIELD OF ECONOMIC
CO-OPERATION   72

The general picture   73

The United Nations Conference on Trade and
Development   75

The United Nations Industrial Development Organisation   78

The United Nations Commission on International Trade
Law   80

Conclusion   85

APPENDICES

1 Preamble, Purposes and Principles of the United
Nations charter   88

2 The Dumbarton Oaks proposals   90

3 The Uniting for Peace resolution   100

4 Resolution 1541 (XV)   104

5 Resolution 1514 (XV)   107

INDEX   109

FOREWORD

By her will, the late Miss Olive Schill of Prestbury, Cheshire, an old friend of the University, whose portrait is painted in Lady Katharine Chorley's *Manchester made them*, left the sum of £10,000 to the University in memory of her brother, Melland Schill, who died in the 1914–18 war. The annual income from this sum is to be used to promote and publish a series of public lectures of the highest possible standard dealing with international law.

The lectures by Miss Gutteridge sum up, in broad lines, the present state of the United Nations, its developments and some of the practical results of its working for now nearly a quarter of a century. They should be of interest to all serious readers and to students of international law and affairs.

Miss Gutteridge is a graduate of Oxford University, a barrister of the Middle Temple, and has spent most of her working life in the legal branch of the Foreign Service. From 1961 to 1964 she was legal adviser to the United Kingdom Permanent Delegation to the United Nations in New York, where, shortly before her retirement from the Foreign Service, she had unique opportunities for seeing the day-to-day working of the United Nations. This book, of course, represents Miss Gutteridge's personal views of the working of the United Nations and its problems and in no way represents the official views of that body or of the Foreign and Commonwealth Office.

Miss Gutteridge is a distinguished daughter of a distinguished father, who was the first Professor of Comparative Law in the University of Cambridge and to whose vision she very properly pays a filial tribute at the end of the lectures.

B. A. WORTLEY

Department of International Law
Law Faculty
University of Manchester

Chapter I

THE CHARTER AS A LIVING DOCUMENT

IN the introduction to his annual report for the years 1958–59 the Secretary-General of the United Nations Organisation—then Dag Hammarskjöld—said: 'The statement of objectives in the charter is binding, and so are the rules concerning the various organs and their competence, but it is not necessary to regard the procedures indicated in the charter as limitative in purpose. They may be supplemented by others under the pressure of circumstances and in the light of experience if these additional procedures are not in conflict with what is prescribed.'[1] It is the purpose of these lectures to consider in general how far the United Nations' charter, which was drawn up to meet the needs of the international community as they were foreseen in 1945, is able without amendment to meet the needs of the greatly expanded international community at the present day; and in relation, specifically, to the maintenance of international peace and security, non-self-governing territories, and certain developments in the field of economic co-operation, to consider what new 'procedures' have been devised, and how far these are consistent both with the Purposes and Principles of the United Nations Organisation as set out in the charter and with express provisions therein designed to give effect to these Purposes and Principles. Foremost among the objectives of the United Nations—as stated in the Preamble to the charter—is the intention 'to save succeeding generations from the scourge of war, which twice in our lifetime has brought untold sorrow to mankind'. However imperfectly this objective has yet been achieved, the growth and development of an Organisation whose first purpose is 'to maintain international peace and security'[2] would appear to be a fitting subject for these lectures, which were founded in memory of Melland Schill, who was one of the many victims of the first world war.

During the period of nearly twenty-five years which has elapsed since the charter was drawn up by the representatives of fifty nations

1

who met at San Francisco in the spring of 1945, the winds of change have blown strongly across the United Nations. The present membership of the new international Organisation which was then created now totals 126, and comprises nearly all the States, both large and small, which are now to be found in the international community. The tendency, already noticeable in the first ten years of the Organisation's life,[3] for its centre of gravity to shift towards the General Assembly—the organ on which all members of the United Nations are represented—has continued. The new Organisation created at San Francisco has had to face, and to attempt to deal with, situations and problems which either did not exist or were not foreseen in 1945, or which it was then hoped, too optimistically, would not occur.

In the first of these categories there must be placed the developments, both civil and military, which have taken place in the field of nuclear energy. At the San Francisco conference the dreadful advent of the atomic bomb was still a few months distant, and the conference therefore discussed the maintenance of international peace and security in the context of armed conflicts conducted with conventional weapons and without any knowledge of the extent to which the possession of nuclear weapons by some of the major powers would complicate the consideration of principles governing disarmament and the regulation of armaments envisaged in article 11, paragraph 1, of the charter.

Another new development, entirely unforeseen at San Francisco, has been the exploration of outer space by two of the major powers, and the consequent need that international law, including the charter of the United Nations, shall 'in the interests of maintaining international peace and security and promoting international co-operation and understanding', apply to all activities in the exploration and use of outer space.[4]

It is, however, the second category—problems and situations not specifically foreseen at San Francisco—which is particularly relevant in the context of the present lectures. In the forefront of this category are questions affecting the maintenance of international peace and security which arise from the fact that it is not so much aggression across international frontiers—the situation leading up to and inherent in the second world war—which is the problem faced by the international community at the present time, but the existence within the boundaries of States of situations which are potentially explosive because of their international implications.

These potentially explosive situations have arisen, in part, out of the emergence of new States, but there are other problems, which do not necessarily threaten international peace and security, which arise from the desire of States which have recently themselves emerged from a colonial or dependent status to bring colonialism in all its forms to an end, and to envisage independence—not merely self-government—as the objective for all dependent territories. Furthermore, these new States are particularly concerned with questions affecting the use and development of their natural resources, and with the existing imbalance between their trade and that of more developed countries.

All these new problems and situations have developed against the background of the breakdown of the wartime co-operation between the Soviet Union and the Western powers, and the ensuing 'cold war'. This has itself led to the lack of unanimity among the permanent members of the Security Council which has, at times, resulted in deadlock. The Organisation has, however, taken steps (which will be examined in more detail in chapter II) to deal with this situation. Partly because those steps were taken, and largely because of the willingness of the States concerned to co-operate, the organisation survived in 1956 a situation—recourse to armed conflict by permanent members of the Security Council—which it was thought, both at San Francisco and immediately afterwards, would lead to the entire disruption of the new Organisation if it occurred.[5] It has also survived the situation created by the fact that one of the permanent members of the Security Council—China—is represented thereon, and at the United Nations in general, by a regime not recognised as a government by many of the member States, and not in control of the mainland of China.

Bearing in mind this general background, I now propose to begin an examination of the general question of the extent to which the evolution of the law of the United Nations is possible without amendment of the charter by a brief, but more specific, indication of the questions which need to be answered in considering how far that law is at present adequate in the three specific fields with which

3

my remaining lectures will deal. These fields, it will be recalled, are, first, the maintenance of international peace and security; second, the problems of non-self-governing territories; and, third, recent developments in economic co-operation.

1. *Maintenance of international peace and security*

In the light of the failure of the League of Nations, it was considered essential at San Francisco to give to an organ of the United Nations —the Security Council—enforcement powers which the Council of the League had never possessed, and to confer on this organ, of which the five great powers are named in the charter as permanent members, the primary responsibility for the maintenance of international peace and security. Chapters VI and VII of the charter deal, respectively, with the powers and functions of the Security Council in relation to the pacific settlement of disputes 'likely to endanger the maintenance of international peace and security', and in relation to threats to the peace, breaches of the peace and acts of aggression.

The questions to be asked here are the following. First, can the Organisation, without amendment of the charter, take action to ensure the maintenance of international peace and security if the Security Council, in any given situation, is unable to act because of lack of unanimity among its permanent members? Second, is the charter adequate, as it now stands, to deal with situations endangering international peace and security which cannot be classified as disputes between States and in which the presence of a United Nations force is required for the purpose of keeping the peace and not for the purpose of coercive action against a State or States?

2. *Non-self-governing territories*

The framers of the charter envisaged the continuance for many years of a situation in which there would be territories whose peoples had not yet achieved a full measure of self-government and which would, therefore, continue to be administered by States which had assumed this responsibility. It is on this premise that chapter XI of the charter was drawn up. The last twenty-five years have, however, seen the emergence from colonial status to independence of a large number of countries, particularly in Africa. These new States are now all members of the United Nations, and consider colonialism in any form to be incompatible with the Purposes and Principles of the United Nations.[6] The questions to be asked here are to what extent certain resolutions adopted by the General Assembly—in particular, resolution 1514 (xv)—can be considered as supplementing the provisions of chapter XI of the charter, and how far these resolutions are consistent with the express provisions of that chapter.

3. *The needs of developing countries*

The rapid growth in the number of new States has led to a distinction, not fully appreciated by if not quite unknown to the framers of the charter, between developed and developing States. The latter need not only economic assistance, but also the opportunity to participate fully in bodies established under the auspices of the United Nations whose purpose is the promotion of international trade in the interests of all States. The question to be considered here is to what extent it is and has been possible to supplement chapter IX of the charter, that is, the chapter which is headed 'International economic and social co-operation'.

The answer to the questions I have posed will depend, to a large extent, on the answer to a more general question. Is the law of the United Nations to be regarded as dynamic or static?

In answer to this question it is possible to adopt widely different standpoints. At one extreme there is a view based on what has been described as the 'teleological principle'.[7] It was stated by Judge Alvarez in the (*First*) *Admissions* case as follows:

... an institution, once established, acquires a life of its own, independent of the elements which have given birth to it, and it must develop, not in accordance with the views of those who created it, but in accordance with the requirements of international life.[8]

At the other extreme is the view which was expressed by Judge Hackworth in his dissenting opinion in the *Injuries* case. Its basic premise is that the powers of the Organisation have been delegated to it by the member States, and that 'such powers as the member States desired to confer upon it are stated either in the charter or in complementary agreements concluded by them' and, consequently, that powers not expressed cannot be freely implied.[9] A similar approach has also been adopted by certain writers on international law, in particular Professor Kelsen. This approach led him to consider in 1951 that certain developments which had occurred in the first five years of the life of the Organisation—including the 'police action' in Korea, and the adoption of the Uniting for Peace resolution by the General Assembly—'may, in some of their aspects, be considered unconstitutional', although they might, at the same time, be regarded as the 'first steps in the development of a new law of the United Nations'.[10]

It appears, however, to be difficult to reconcile the extreme view—that is, the view based on the premise that the only powers the Organisation can exercise are those specifically delegated to it in the charter—with the acceptance of the Organisation as an international person. In its advisory opinion in the *Injuries* case, the International Court of Justice held that

... the organisation was intended to exercise and enjoy, and is in fact exercising and enjoying, functions and rights which can be explained only on the basis of the possession of a large measure of international personality and the capacity to operate upon an international plane. It could not carry out the intentions of its founders if it was devoid of international personality. .... It must be acknowledged that its members, by entrusting certain functions to it, with the attendant duties and responsibilities, have clothed it with the competence required to enable those functions to be effectively discharged.

Accordingly, the Court has come to the conclusion that the Organisation is an international person.[11]

Furthermore, the Court went on to say that

Under international law, the organisation must be deemed to have those powers which, though not expressly provided in the charter, are conferred upon it by necessary implication as being essential to the performance of its duties.[12]

The views which the International Court had expressed in the *Injuries* case as to the nature of the powers possessed by the Organisation underlay its later opinion in the *Certain Expenses* case which will be considered in more detail in my second lecture. The Court as a whole did not, however, appear to go quite as far as Sir Percy Spender in his separate opinion in the latter case. He approached the teleological concept of charter interpretation when he said that it

was intended to apply to varying conditions in a changing and evolving world community and to a multiplicity of unpredictable situations and events. Its provisions were intended to adjust themselves to the ever changing pattern of international existence. .... The stated purposes of the charter should be the prime consideration in interpreting the text.[13]

The dynamic, as contrasted to the static, view of the United Nations and its charter has been supported by many writers on international law during the present lifetime of the Organisation. Writing in 1946, and comparing the charter with the covenant of the League of Nations, the late Professor Brierly asserted the evolutionary view when he said:

Constitutions always have to be interpreted and applied and in the process they are overlaid with precedents and conventions which change them, after a time, into something very different from what anyone, with only the original text before him, could possibly have foreseen.[14]

This conception of a 'perpetual transformation' has been elaborated by other writers in examining, in particular, developments within the area of the maintenance of international peace and security. Speaking of the Uniting for Peace resolution, Andrassy has written:

As to the legal aspects, the resolution is undoubtedly a step in the evolution of the law of the United Nations. ... Every new disposition, every resolution of the General Assembly elaborating in more detail the provisions of the charter and other sources of the law of the United Nations adds new elements to that law. The same is the effect of the practice, the day to day application of the charter.[15]

Both Seyersted and Bowett, writing on United Nations forces, have adopted the dynamic rather than the static view. Bowett says, for instance, that

It has generally come to be acknowledged that international constitutional instruments are to be interpreted dynamically and that the powers of an international organisation may go beyond those specifically allocated to it.[16]

Seyersted, writing rather earlier, was clearly of the same view when he wrote that 'the capacity of international organisations is not confined to such acts or rights as are specified in their constitutions'.[17]

That the United Nations itself is in favour of the dynamic rather than the static approach to the law of the charter is evident from the establishment by General Assembly resolution 1815 (XVII), adopted on 18 December 1962, of a Special Committee on Principles of International Law concerning Friendly Relations and Co-operation among States which is charged with the task of studying certain basic principles of the charter, and eventually reporting upon them and recommending ways in which they can be progressively developed. The Special Committee has now had three sessions, the last at the time of writing, being from 9 to 30 September 1968. One of its problems is to meet the desires of the new States to play a leading role in the progressive development of international law by elaborating in more detail certain provisions of the charter, and at the same time to avoid giving those provisions meanings they were not intended to bear—for example, by interpreting article 2 (4) of the charter as applying to the use of economic coercion as well as to the use of armed force.

To adopt the dynamic, as opposed to the static, view of charter interpretation is not therefore necessarily to hold that clear provisions of the charter can be altered at will, or that, without amendment of the charter, the United Nations has an entirely unlimited capacity for growth and development. It is submitted that the test of the legal validity of any new development, and of any action by the Organisation or one of its organs which is not specifically provided for in the charter, is a double one: the action or development must not be precluded by any express provisions of the charter, and it must be action which is necessary to carry out the Purposes of the Organisation as these are set out in article 1 of the charter. It is also submitted that the General Assembly cannot automatically validate any development or action which does not satisfy this two-fold test merely by voting in favour of it. It will be remembered that in his separate opinion in the *Certain Expenses* case, Sir Gerald Fitzmaurice raised the question of whether the General Assembly has the power automatically to validate expenditure of any kind whatsoever incurred by the Organisation simply by voting for it. He concluded that if the answer was in the affirmative 'a degree of power—if not unlimited, certainly much greater than was ever contemplated in the framing of the charter—would be placed in the hands of the Assembly'.[18] This would seem to be equally true of other kinds of action taken by the Organisation.

On the other hand, the static rather than the dynamic approach to the evolution of the law of the charter limits the opportunities for legitimate growth and change. Many of the recent developments in the United Nations would, if the static approach were adopted, probably be considered to lack constitutional validity until there were a change in the charter. This would be a discouraging prospect, since there is at present little possibility of making use of the formal procedure for revision set out in chapter XVIII of the charter. Few would dispute that although 'it is desirable to review the charter in the light of experience gained in its operation', the corollary, which is stated in the preamble to General Assembly resolution 992 (x), that 'such a review should be conducted under auspicious international circumstances' is as true in 1969 as it was in 1955. To illustrate the importance of this political factor, it is necessary to consider briefly the procedures set out in articles 108 and 109 of the charter, and the extent to which they have been invoked or used during the first twenty-five years of the life of the Organisation.

Under article 108, amendments to the charter come into force for all members of the United Nations when they have been adopted by a vote of two-thirds of the members of the General Assembly and ratified, in accordance with their respective constitutional processes, by two-thirds of the members of the United Nations, including all the permanent members of the Security Council.[19] Under article 109, a general conference of the members of the United Nations for the purpose of reviewing the charter may be held at a date and place to be fixed by a two-thirds vote of the members of the General Assembly and by a vote of any seven members of the Security Council. Any alteration of the charter recommended by a two-thirds vote of the conference is to take effect when ratified in accordance with their respective constitutional processes by two-thirds of the members of the United Nations, including all the permanent members of the Security Council. Furthermore, if such a conference has not been held before the tenth annual session of the General Assembly following the entry into force of the charter, the proposal to call such a conference is to be placed on the agenda of that session, and the conference is to be held if so decided by a majority vote of the members of the General Assembly and by a vote of any seven members of the Security Council.

The conference provided for in Article 109 of the charter has never been held. In accordance with the provisions of its third paragraph, the proposal to call a general conference was placed on the agenda of the tenth session of the General Assembly, but the upshot of this was the adoption of a resolution—992 (x)—by which the Assembly, after deciding that 'a general conference to review the charter shall be held at an appropriate time', appointed a committee consisting of all members of the United Nations to consider, in consultation with the Secretary-General, the question of fixing a time and place for the conference, and its organisation and procedures, and to report with its recommendations to the General Assembly at its twelfth session.

Consideration by the General Assembly of this report merely led to a decision—in resolution 1136 (xii)—to keep the committee in being, and to request it to report to the Assembly at its fourteenth session. The life of the committee was prolonged by successive resolutions of the General Assembly,[20] but for several years nothing further was done. It is little wonder that, as a somewhat wry joke, the committee began to be known in the corridors of the United Nations as the Committee for Not Reviewing the Charter. There was, however, at last a breakthrough. When the committee reported to the General Assembly at the eighteenth session it had organised a comprehensive consultation of the delegations of member States as a result of which specific recommendations were made for amending those provisions of the charter which relate to the number of seats in the Security Council and in the Economic and Social Council. These recommendations, which also took into account a resolution of the Economic and Social Council urging the General Assembly to bring about an appropriate increase in the membership of the Economic and Social Council, were made in the light of the large increase in the membership of the United Nations since 1946, and the widespread feeling amongst the newer members that the composition of the Security Council was 'inequitable and unbalanced', and that both in the case of the Security Council and that of the Economic and Social Council a more adequate geographical distribution would enable each organ to carry out more effectively its respective functions under the charter. It should be noted, however, that the proposed increase in the membership of the Security Council related only to the number of the non-permanent members.

As the result of these recommendations, the General Assembly at its eighteenth session adopted resolution 1991 (xviii). In this resolution it decided to adopt, in accordance with article 108 of the charter, amendments to articles 23, 27 and 61 of the charter. The amendments to article 23 have the effect of increasing the number of the non-permanent members of the Security Council from six to ten, and the total membership of the Security Council from eleven to fifteen; those to article 27 substitute nine for seven as the number of affirmative votes required under paragraphs 2 and 3. The amendment to article 61 increases the membership of the Economic and Social Council from eighteen to twenty-seven, and makes other amendments to the text of article 61 consequential on the increase in membership.

The amendments adopted by the General Assembly in resolution 1991 (XVIII) entered into force on 31 August 1965 in accordance with article 108,[21] as did on 12 June 1968 a consequential amendment to article 109 of the charter which substitutes nine for seven as the number of members of the Security Council required to convene a general conference for the purpose of revising the charter.[22] This amendment was considered by the sixth committee at the twentieth session of the General Assembly, and was adopted by the Assembly in resolution 2101 (XX)

Up to the time of writing, these are the only amendments to the charter of the United Nations which have been adopted. It will be noted that they are all of a 'numerical' character, and concern changes which, on any possible view of the evolution of the law of the charter, could not have been made in practice without infringing specific provisions of the charter.

We have therefore still with us the situation referred to by Professor Kelsen in 1951—the situation in which it is difficult, if not entirely impossible, to put into operation the amendment procedures for which the charter expressly provides. In these circumstances there exists, as Kelsen himself recognised,[23] the need for the law of the charter to adapt itself to changing circumstances by accepting interpretations of the charter which, although they may be more or less consistent with the letter of the law, may not be in conformity with the ascertainable intentions of the authors of the charter.

These lectures are, however, based on an assumption which is of a more dynamic and evolutionary character. This is the assumption that subject to the essential limitation—conformity with express provisions of the charter and the functions and purposes of the Organisation as specified in the charter—the United Nations Organisation is legally capable of growth and development to meet needs of the international community which were unforeseen when the

11

charter was drawn up in 1945, and is legally competent to deal with situations which were then either not envisaged at all or were imperfectly appreciated. If this assumption is accepted there is less cause to be troubled by the difficulty alluded to by Kelsen of reconciling the principle *ex injuria jus non oritur*—law cannot originate in an illegal act—with the need to adapt the law of the charter to changed circumstances.

It still remains necessary, however, to examine all new developments in the light of the test I have suggested. The application of this test appears, indeed, to be more than ever necessary at the present time, when the General Assembly has a tendency, which has been noted recently both by its Secretary-General and by the President of the Assembly,[24] to adopt emotional resolutions. Not only is it a fact that 'the evils of the world are not cured simply by negotiating resolutions', but the law of the charter cannot develop as the result of resolutions adopted by the General Assembly if these disregard existing provisions of the charter or go beyond the Purposes and Principles of the Organisation as stated in the charter. I cannot, within the compass of these lectures, examine all recent developments at the United Nations, and I have deliberately excluded consideration of such issues as Rhodesia and South West Africa. Both these situations are *sui generis*, but if they are examined in detail it is, of course, none the less important to apply to the measures the Organisation has taken to deal with them the test to which I have referred.

In the following lectures I shall examine in much greater detail the legal capacity of the United Nations in relation to the three subjects I referred to at the beginning of this lecture: the maintenance of international peace and security; non-self-governing territories; and developments in the field of economic co-operation.

NOTES

[1] *Introduction to the annual report of the Secretary-General, 1958–59,* p. 2 (G.A.O.R., fourteenth session, supplement No. 1A).

[2] See Appendix 1 for the United Nations' charter, *Preamble, Purposes and Principles.*

[3] See, for instance, Vallat: *Voting in the General Assembly of the United Nations,* B.Y.B.I.L., 1954, p. 271; Jennings: *The progress of international law,* B.Y.B.I.L., 1958, p. 349.

[4] Article III of the Treaty on Principles Governing the Activities of States in the Exploration and Use of Outer Space, including the Moon and other Celestial Bodies, United Kingdom Treaty Series, No. 10 (1968). This article of the treaty, and its other provisions, are discussed by Fawcett: *International law and the uses of outer space*, Manchester University Press, 1968. This book is the published version of the 1968 Melland Schill lectures.

[5] In the official British commentary on the charter, published soon after this entry into force, it is said: 'It is ... clear that no enforcement action by the Organisation can be taken against a great power itself without a major war. If such a situation arises, the United Nations will have failed in its purpose and all members will have to act as seems best in the circumstances. ...'

[6] Representatives of such States at the United Nations refer, for example, to 'the liberation of peoples' as a charter principle (A/6700. Add. 5, p. 13) and have rejected the customary rules of international law concerning colonies and protectorates (Prakash Sinha: *Perspective of the newly independent States on the binding quality of international law*, I.C.L.Q., vol. 14, p. 122).

[7] Fitzmaurice: *The law and procedure of the International Court of Justice*, B.Y.B.I.L., 1952, pp. 5–6.

[8] I.C.J. reports, 1948, p. 68.

[9] I.C.J. reports, 1950, p. 198.

[10] Kelsen: *Recent trends in the law of the United Nations*, Stevens & Sons, 1951, p. 912.

[11] I.C.J. reports, 1949, p. 178.

[12] *Ibid*, p. 182.

[13] I.C.J. reports, 1962, p. 185.

[14] Brierly: *The Covenant and the Charter*, B.Y.B.I.L., 1946, p. 83.

[15] Andrassy: *Uniting for peace*, A.J.I.L., 1950, p. 582.

[16] Bowett: *United Nations Forces*, pp. 307–8.

[17] Seyersted: *United Nations forces*, B.Y.B.I.L., 1961, p. 453.

[18] I.C.J. reports, 1962, p. 203.

[19] Article 108 is based on chapter XI of the Dumbarton Oaks proposals, which, however, provided for ratification of amendments by the permanent members of the Security Council, and a *majority* (not two-thirds, as in article 108) of the other members of the organisation. Article 108 can be contrasted with article 26 of the covenant of the League of Nations, under which amendments to the covenant were to take effect when ratified by the members of the League whose representatives composed the Council, and a majority of the other members of the League. A significant difference, however, is that article 26 also provides that no amendment so adopted 'shall bind any member of the League which signifies its dissent therefrom, but in that case it shall cease to be a member of the League'.

[20] Resolutions 1381 (XIV), 1670 (XVI) and 1756 (XVII).

[21] Protocol of Entry into Force: United Kingdom Treaty Series No. 2 (1966). For a more detailed discussion of these amendments and their legislative history see Schwelb: *Amendments to Articles 23, 27 and 61 of the Charter*. A.J.I.L., 1965, pp. 834–50; and *The 1963–65 amendments to the Charter of the United Nations*, A.J.I.L., 1966, pp. 371–8.

[22] Protocol of Entry into Force: United Kingdom Treaty Series No. 5 (1969). See also Schwelb's note in A.J.I.L., 1966 (*loc. cit.*).

[23] Kelsen: *Recent trends in the law of the United Nations*, p. 911.

[24] *The Times*, 22 December 1968.

Chapter II

THE MAINTENANCE OF INTERNATIONAL PEACE AND SECURITY

(1) UNITING FOR PEACE

IT is sometimes forgotten nowadays that the United Nations charter, in embryo, is to be found in the Dumbarton Oaks proposals (see Appendix 2). These proposals were published on 9 October 1944 under the auspices of four sponsoring governments—those of the United Kingdom, the United States, the Soviet Union and China. Their purpose was to provide a scheme for 'a general international organisation under the title of the United Nations' which could later be discussed at a full conference of those allied and associated powers who were already known as the United Nations.[1] The intention of the sponsoring governments in formulating these proposals was to remedy what, in the light of the circumstances leading up to the second world war, appeared to be grave defects in the covenant of the League of Nations, and in particular what appeared to be its fundamental weaknesses—the absence of effective collective arrangements for the maintenance of international peace and security, and the ultimate freedom of a member State to use force to effect a settlement.

As regards the first defect, although both the League Council (under article 4 of the covenant) and the League Assembly (under article 3) could deal with 'any matter within the sphere of action of the League or affecting the peace of the world', the League lacked any central machinery for enforcing the decision of either organ. Although, as has been stated,[2] the 'authors of the covenant started from the idea that all members of the League were equally bound to participate in sanctions', and although each member undertook immediately to subject any member of the League resorting to war in breach of articles 12, 13 and 15 of the covenant to the economic sanctions prescribed in the first paragraph of article 16, there was no explicit provision in the covenant that the Council of the League should determine whether a situation calling for the application of

14

sanctions existed, and such determination was therefore left to the individual judgment of member States. Nor, in the event of a member of the League resorting to war, had the Council power to do more than 'to recommend to the several governments concerned what effective military, naval or air force the members of the League shall severally contribute to the armed forces to be used to protect the covenants of the League'.[3] There was therefore under the Covenant no central organ 'with powers to determine with effect binding upon all members the occasions for the obligatory collective use of force'[4] and endowed with executive powers of enforcement action.

As regards the second defect referred to above, although under article 12 of the covenant the members of the League agreed that 'if there should arise between them any dispute likely to lead to a rupture' they would submit the matter either to arbitration or to inquiry by the Council, they did not, even under that article, agree to outlaw resort to war as an ultimate means of settlement. They did, however, agree not to resort to war until three months after an award by arbitrators or a report by the Council of the League, and to be subject both to a further restriction under article 13, which bound them not to resort to war against a member of the League which complied with an arbitral award, and to their undertaking, contained in article 15, not to go to war with any party to a dispute which complied with recommendations of the Council made under that article. Under the Dumbarton Oaks proposals, however, it was the intention to prohibit, not simply 'resort to war', but the threat or use of force in any manner inconsistent with the purposes of the new organisation contemplated by those proposals. This intention is fully carried out in article 2, paragraph 4, of the charter, which provides that:

All members shall refrain in their international relations from the threat or use of force against the territorial integrity or political independence of any State, or in any other manner inconsistent with the Purposes of the United Nations.

The charter therefore goes a good deal further than the covenant in outlawing the use of force as an instrument of national policy, and its other provisions—in particular, chapter VII, which is based on chapter VIII B of the Dumbarton Oaks proposals and is headed

'Action with respect to threats to the peace, breaches of the peace and acts of aggression'—must be considered in the light of this significant advance.

Bearing in mind the deficiencies in the covenant, and the fact that the first purpose of the new organisation was to be the maintenance of international peace and security, it is not surprising to find in chapter VI of the Dumbarton Oaks proposals the concept of a security council on which members of the new organisation would confer primary responsibility for the maintenance of international peace and security and which would not consist (as in the case of the Council of the League) of *all* members of the organisation, but of eleven members only, of whom five should have permanent seats. Nor is it surprising to find in chapter VIII B of the Dumbarton Oaks proposals the provisions which, with very few changes, are now embodied in chapter VII of the charter.

In contrast to the covenant of the League of Nations, the charter, in chapter VII, provides that it is the Council which is to determine the existence of any threat to the peace, breach of the peace or act of aggression, and if necessary to *decide upon* (not merely to recommend to member States) what measures are to be taken to maintain or restore international peace and security. Whilst the intention of the covenant had been to create a system of co-operation between States who agreed to do or not to do certain things in the exercise of their sovereignty, there was hardly anything which the League, as an organisation, could do; on the other hand, the charter clearly envisages the purposes of the United Nations as being those of the Organisation as a corporate body, and not simply those of its members severally.[5]

What is contemplated in chapter VII of the charter, if diplomatic, economic or other measures not involving the use of armed force prove to be inadequate, is combined international enforcement action based on national contingents provided by member States. For this purpose, under article 43 of the charter, special agreements are to be negotiated 'on the initiative of the Security Council' and concluded between the Council and individual members or groups of members.[6] Thus the charter, as a whole, but chapter VII in particular, was intended to remedy one of the gravest deficiencies in the covenant —the inability of the League itself to take military measures to prevent or suppress aggression. Hence the emphasis on enforcement measures and centralised control of action by armed forces.[7]

In presenting the report of committee III/3 on chapter VIII B of the Dumbarton Oaks proposals—ultimately chapter VII of the United Nations' charter—the rapporteur summarised the results in the following terms:

This part of the proposals of Dumbarton Oaks constitutes . . . from the point of view of security, definite and considerable progress over measures adopted previously and especially over the covenant of the League of Nations . . . Military assistance, in case of aggression, ceases to be a 'recommendation' made to member States; it becomes for us an *obligation* which none can shirk. If these proposals are adopted, the international organisation will cease to be unarmed in the face of violence; a collective force the size, the degree of preparedness, the composition, and the general location of which will be determined beforehand will have been placed at the disposal of the Council to carry out their decisions.[8]

Realisation of this optimistic forecast depended in the main on two factors: unanimity of the permanent members of the Security Council in the event of a threat to the peace, breach of the peace or act of aggression, and the readiness of member States 'to make available to the Security Council, on its call and in accordance with a special agreement or agreements, armed forces, assistance and facilities . . . necessary for the purpose of maintaining international peace and security' (article 43 of the charter). Moreover, implicit in the rapporteur's statement is the belief that the situations the new organisation would have to face would be broadly the same as those which had confronted the League of Nations, that is, situations calling for coercive action against a particular State or governmental authority. The long discussions at San Francisco of chapters VIII, sections A and B, of the Dumbarton Oaks proposals—ultimately chapters VI and VII of the charter—do not disclose any realisation that the new organisation might need to take collective action involving the use of armed forces which would be neither coercive nor directed against a particular State but which would have as its aim the maintenance of international peace and security.

The purpose of this and the following lecture is to examine what steps the Organisation has taken to deal with situations in which the Security Council is unable to act to maintain international peace and security owing to lack of unanimity among the permanent members of the Council, and what steps it has taken to keep the peace in situations unforeseen and thus unprovided for by the drafters of the charter. These two aspects of peace-keeping cannot be dealt with entirely separately, since both are affected by the view, consistently maintained by the Soviet Union, that the only circumstances in which the organisation may legally use armed forces are those foreseen and expressly provided for in chapter VII of the charter.

Two factors in particular have contributed to situations in which it has been difficult, if not entirely impossible, for the Organisation to take the coercive action provided for in chapter VII. These are (1) the absence of 'special agreements' under article 43, and (2) the lack of unanimity of the permanent members of the Security Council.

1. THE ABSENCE OF 'SPECIAL AGREEMENTS' UNDER ARTICLE 43

Opinions differ as to whether other provisions of chapter VII, in particular article 42, can be invoked in the absence of the special agreements provided for in article 43 of the charter.[9] There will continue to be argument about this, but it is, of course, a fact that the kind of special agreement contemplated in article 43 has never been concluded, and that article 43 remains a dead letter. It is not always realised, however, that in the early years of the life of the Organisation, the Military Staff Committee (constituted under article 47 of the charter) was entrusted by the Security Council with the task of drawing up 'general principles governing the organisation of the armed forces made available to the Security Council by member nations of the United Nations', and that it produced a set of draft articles which were provisionally approved by the Security Council in June 1947. These draft articles were, however, never finally approved, owing to differences of opinion between the Military Staff Committee and the Council about such matters as the composition and size of the force to be provided under such agreements.[10]

2. THE LACK OF UNANIMITY OF THE PERMANENT MEMBERS
OF THE SECURITY COUNCIL

Chapter VI of the Dumbarton Oaks proposals, which corresponds to chapter V of the charter, has no provisions corresponding to article 27 of the charter, but merely a note stating that 'the question of voting procedure in the Security Council is still under consideration'. The voting formula which now appears in article 27 was first settled at

Yalta on 11 February 1945, by the USSR, the United States and the United Kingdom, and was later assented to by China and France. This formula was discussed at length at San Francisco.[11] Twenty-three questions on it were submitted by other delegations to those of the sponsoring governments, and proposals for its amendment were made.[12] The formula nevertheless emerged unchanged and is now article 27 of the charter. In the present context it is paragraph 3 which is important, and this as adopted read as follows:

Decisions of the Security Council on all other matters [that is, on all non-procedural matters] shall be made by an affirmative vote of seven members including the concurring votes of the permanent members; provided that in decisions under chapter VI, and under paragraph 3 of article 52, a party to a dispute shall abstain from voting.

This paragraph has subsequently been amended by the substitution of 'nine' for 'seven' in consequence of other amendments increasing the size of the Security Council; otherwise it remains unchanged.[13] Although the Security Council has in practice consistently interpreted the words 'including the concurring votes of the permanent members' as meaning that only a negative vote by a permanent member, and not merely absence or an abstention, will prevent the adoption of a non-procedural motion which has obtained the necessary seven (now nine) votes, the desire expressed at an early stage by the General Assembly that all permanent members of the Security Council would show restraint in the use of the veto[14] has not been met, since the Soviet Union has exercised its right of veto on more than a hundred occasions. Although the absence of the representative of the Soviet Union from the Security Council in June and July 1950 enabled the Council to take action to deal with 'the armed attack upon the Republic of Korea by forces from North Korea', the return of the Soviet representative in the following month frustrated any further action by the Security Council. This situation led to the adoption by the General Assembly on 3 November 1950 of the 'Uniting for Peace' resolution.

THE UNITING FOR PEACE RESOLUTION[15]

The resolution (see Appendix 3) is divided into five parts: of these probably the best known is part A, and it is the one which relates most directly to the situation in Korea which gave birth to the resolution. The General Assembly thereby resolved:

19

that if the Security Council, because of lack of unanimity of the permanent members, fails to exercise its primary responsibility for the maintenance of international peace and security in any case where there appears to be a threat to the peace, breach of the peace or act of aggression, the General Assembly shall consider the matter immediately with a view to making appropriate recommendations to members for collective measures, including in the case of a breach of the peace or act of aggression the use of armed force, when necessary, to maintain or restore international peace and security.

Under part B of the resolution the General Assembly established a Peace Observation Commission, and under part D a Collective Measures Committee. The Peace Observation Commission was intended to 'observe and report on the situation in any area where there exists international tension the continuance of which is likely to endanger the maintenance of international peace and security'. The General Assembly 'may utilise the Commission if the Security Council is not exercising the functions assigned to it by the charter' 'upon the invitation or with the consent of the State into whose territory the Commission would go'. The Collective Measures Committee, consisting of fourteen members,[16] was, in consultation with the Secretary-General and member States, to study and make a report on 'methods . . . which might be used to maintain and strengthen international peace and security in accordance with the Purposes and Principles of the charter, taking account of collective self-defence and regional arrangements'. Amongst the methods to be studied were those envisaged in part C of the resolution, which recommended

to the States members of the United Nations that each member maintains within its national armed forces elements so trained, organised and equipped that they could promptly be made available, in accordance with its constitutional processes, for service as a United Nations unit or units, upon recommendation by the Security Council or the General Assembly, without prejudice to the use of such elements in exercise of the right of individual or collective self-defence recognised in article 51 of the charter.

From the time of the debates on the resolution in the General Assembly up to the present day, opinion has been sharply divided as to the legality, and, in particular, the conformity with the charter, of the Uniting for Peace resolution. It is, of course, true that the charter makes no specific provision for the case in which action by the Security Council is blocked 'because of lack of unanimity of the permanent members'. It is also true that 'the resolution envisages steps being taken on the initiative of the Assembly that may not have been contemplated by those who drafted the charter'.[17] It is indeed possible to go further and to point out that committee III/3 of the San Francisco conference referred in its report to proposals for participation of the Assembly in decisions relating to enforcement measures, and that the report stated that the 'application of enforcement measures, in order to be effective, must above all be swift' and concluded that it was 'impossible to conceive of swift and effective action if decisions of the Council must be submitted to ratification by the Assembly, or if the measures applied by the Council are susceptible of revision by the Assembly'.[18] But such proposals, it must be noted, referred to ratification or revision of the Council's decisions by the General Assembly, and not to the situation in which, because of lack of unanimity of the permanent members, the Council has failed to take a decision. More relevant, in the context of the Uniting for Peace resolution, is the committee's observation that to provide for the participation of the General Assembly in decisions relating to enforcement measures 'would be contrary to the basic idea of the Organisation, which contemplated a differentiation between the functions of the Council and those of the Assembly'.[19]

· It is now necessary to examine in more detail the grounds which have been advanced for contesting the legality of the Uniting for Peace resolution. The first ground is that it is the Security Council which is exclusively entitled to take action for the maintenance of international peace and security. On that view the General Assembly may discuss and make recommendations about problems relating to the maintenance of peace and security, but cannot go beyond that. Therefore any action by the General Assembly (e.g. the establishment under section B of part A of the Uniting for peace resolution of a peace observation commission, or the establishment of a collective measures committee under section D) which goes beyond the making of a recommendation is, according to this view, *ultra vires* the General Assembly.

The validity or otherwise of this view rests on the interpretation of the second paragraph of article 11 of the charter, and in particular its last sentence. This paragraph reads as follows:

The General Assembly may discuss any questions relating to the maintenance of international peace and security brought before it by any member of the United Nations, or by the Security Council, or by a State which is not a member of the United Nations, in accordance with article 35, paragraph 2, and, except as provided in article 12, may make recommendations with regard to any such questions to the State or States concerned or to the Security Council or to both. Any such question on which action is necessary shall be referred to the Security Council by the General Assembly either before or after discussion.

The reference to article 12 is to its first paragraph, which provides that 'While the Security Council is exercising in respect of any dispute or situation the functions assigned to it in the present charter, the General Assembly shall not make any recommendation with regard to that dispute or situation unless the Security Council so requests.'

The International Court of Justice dealt with the interpretation of the last sentence of paragraph 2 of article 11 of the charter in its advisory opinion on *Certain expenses of the United Nations*.[20] It is important to bear in mind, however, that the Court was not asked to consider whether the Uniting for Peace resolution was in conformity with the charter, but whether certain expenditures which were authorised by the General Assembly to cover the cost of the United Nations operations in the Congo, and the operations of UNEF in the Middle East, constituted 'expenses of the Organisation' within the meaning of paragraph 2 of article 17 of the charter. In this context, however, the Court had to consider the argument that 'one type of expenses, namely those resulting from operations for the maintenance of international peace and security are not "expenses of the Organisation within the meaning of article 17, paragraph 2 ... inasmuch as they fall to be dealt with exclusively by the Security Council, and more especially through agreements negotiated in accordance with article 43". This argument, the Court said, "rests in part on the view that when the maintenance of international peace and security is involved, it is only the Security Council which is authorised to decide on any action relative thereto".'[21]

The Court rejected this argument in the following passage of its opinion:

The Court considers that the kind of action referred to in article 11, paragraph 2, is coercive or enforcement action. This paragraph applies not merely to general questions relating to peace and security but also to specific cases brought before the General Assembly by a State under article 35 and empowers the General Assembly by means of recommendations to States or to the Security Council, or to both, to organise peacekeeping operations at the request, or with the consent, of the State concerned. This power of the General Assembly is a special power which in no way derogates from its general powers under article 10 or article 14 except as limited by the last sentence of article 11, paragraph 2 . . . The last sentence of article 11, paragraph 2, has no application where the necessary action is not enforcement action.[22]

Sir Gerald Fitzmaurice endorsed this view when he said in his separate opinion: 'Enforcement or coercitive action *stricto sensu* is . . . exclusively for the Security Council, but the action of the Assembly in the Middle East and in the Congo has not been of this character.'[23] On the other hand, Judge Koretsky in his dissenting opinion said that 'under the charter, only the Security Council may take any action with regard to a question relating to the maintenance of international peace and security'.[24] In his view a mere recommendation by the General Assembly would not constitute 'action', and he illustrated this by saying that the General Assembly 'may, for example, recommend a cease-fire, but it cannot set up the United Nations force and decide to bring it into an area of military conflict in order to provide the implementation of the cease fire'.[25] On this view it would seem that, while recommendation to members under part A of the Uniting for Peace resolution for 'collective measures . . . to maintain or restore international peace or security' might not be *ultra vires* the Assembly, any action by the Assembly to coordinate these measures would be contrary to the charter.

The second argument against the legality of the Uniting for Peace resolution, which is closely connected with the first, is that the resolution has, in regard to the maintenance of international peace and security, transferred the centre of gravity of the United Nations to the General Assembly, or—to put it another way—that the General Assembly is usurping powers which belong exclusively to the Security Council. This view was expressed by Judge Koretsky, although not specifically in the context of the Uniting for Peace resolution, when he said in his dissenting opinion in the *Certain Expenses* case that: 'To place the Security Council . . . beside the General Assembly, considering them as interchangeable in solving and implementing the tasks of maintaining international peace and security, would be objectively to replace the Security Council by the General Assembly, to put the Council aside and thereby undermine the very foundations of the Organisation.'[26] This argument appears to disregard that under the charter the primary purpose of the Organisation as a whole is to keep the peace. Moreover, 'the charter . . . attempts to implement and not to stultify international obligations'; even if it is considered that the veto can render any action under the charter impossible, action may still be possible under ordinary international law.[27]

But even those who take a more liberal view than Judge Koretsky of the meaning of the word 'action' in paragraph 2 of article 11 of the charter, and are prepared to admit that, on one interpretation, although others are possible, it means only action under chapter VII of the charter, still doubt the legality of the General Assembly determining the existence of a threat to the peace, breach of the peace or act of aggression. Kelsen, for instance, considers that under the charter the power to make such a determination is conferred only on the Security Council.[28] Another respect in which it has been alleged that the resolution is inconsistent with, even if not actually contrary, to, the charter is that it duplicates procedures and mechanisms which, under the charter, are at the exclusive disposal of the Security Council. For instance, the Collective Measures Committee appears to be in some respects a duplicate of the Military Staff Committee for which chapter VII of the charter provides.

As has already been seen, the International Court of Justice expressly rejected the argument, based on the last sentence of paragraph 2 of article 11 of the charter, that the General Assembly could take no action going beyond the making of recommendations for the maintenance of international peace and security, and considered that the kind of action referred to in that sentence is coercive or enforcement action. On the basis that the Court meant coercive or enforcement action, *stricto sensu*, this part of its opinion does not imply that collective measures involving the use of armed force recommended by the General Assembly under part A of the Uniting for Peace resolution would always and necessarily be unconstitutional.

The arguments against the legality of the resolution have, in the period of nearly twenty years which has elapsed since its adoption, been considered by a number of writers on international law. There are those, like Kelsen, who doubt its legality basically because their view of the law of the charter, and hence of the possibilities of its evolution, is not a dynamic one. Others, however, make the following points in support of their view that the Uniting for Peace resolution is not contrary to the charter:

(a) Under article 24 of the charter, the Security Council has the *primary*, not the exclusive, responsibility for the maintenance of international peace and security. Even at the stage of the Dumbarton Oaks proposals, some overlapping was contemplated, and at San Francisco a new provision—article 10 of the charter—was added which, by enabling the General Assembly to 'discuss any questions or any matters within the scope of the charter' and, except as provided in article 12, to make recommendations thereon, gave to the Assembly a wide concurrence of functions with the Security Council.[29]

(b) On the basis that the last sentence of paragraph 2 of article 11 of the charter relates only to enforcement action, and bearing in mind that part A of the Uniting for Peace resolution does not enable the Assembly to decide upon collective measures, but only to recommend them, the resolution grants the General Assembly no greater powers than it already has under articles 10 and 11 (2) of the charter.[30]

(c) The machinery for the maintenance of international peace and security set up by the Uniting for Peace resolution was intended to improve and reinforce the machinery of the United Nations for preserving peace, and not to supplant the Security Council.[31]

(d) The Uniting for Peace resolution contemplates action based on articles 10, 11 (2) and 14 of the charter. It recognises that some kinds of procedure are not open to the Assembly, notably the power to make legally binding orders on members to participate in collective measures.[32]

Unless the view is taken that nothing can be done under the charter which is not specifically provided for therein, a good case can be made out for the legality of the Uniting for Peace resolution. It is fully consistent with the Purposes and Principles of the United Nations as set out in article 1 (1) of the charter, and it does not

C 25

purport in any way to supersede chapter VII of the charter, nor to confer on the General Assembly any power to take the mandatory decisions that are reserved for the Security Council under that chapter. Above all, it recognises, as is stated in one of its preambular paragraphs, that the failure of the Security Council to discharge its responsibilities on behalf of all the member States does not relieve those States of their obligations, or the United Nations of its responsibility under the charter, to maintain international peace and security.

NOTES

[1] The Dumbarton Oaks proposals were preceded by the Atlantic Charter of 14 August 1941; the Declaration by the 'United Nations' of 1 January 1942; and by a Declaration signed on behalf of the United States, the United Kingdom and the Soviet Union on 30 October 1943 which expressly recognised the necessity of a general international organisation, based on sovereign equality, for the maintenance of international peace and security.

[2] Lalive: *International organisations and neutrality*, B.Y.B.I.L., 1947, p. 73.

[3] Article 16 of the Covenant of the League of Nations.

[4] Oppenheim: *International law* (seventh edition), vol II, p. 173.

[5] Brierly: *The Covenant and the Charter*, B.Y.B.I.L., 1946, pp. 84–6.

[6] The Dumbarton Oaks proposals (chapter VIII B, paragraph 5) envisaged special agreements of this type *between members* and requiring only the *approval* of the Security Council.

[7] In this context it is interesting to note that article 51 of the charter, which appears in chapter VII and preserves 'the inherent right of individual or collective self-defence', was not among the corresponding Dumbarton Oaks proposals, but was added at San Francisco.

[8] U.N.C.I.O., vol. 12, p. 513.

[9] These arguments are examined by Seyersted: *United Nations Forces*, B.Y.B.I.L., 1961, pp. 438–9.

[10] Seyersted, *loc. cit.*, pp. 360–2, Bowett: *United Nations Forces*, pp. 12–18.

[11] U.N.C.I.O., vol. 11, pp. 309–10; 694–8.

[12] *Ibid*, pp. 694–8. These included a proposal (not accepted) that 'all decisions involving the use of armed force to maintain the peace' should be taken by four-fifths of the permanent members and three-quarters of the non-permanent members.

[13] General Assembly resolution 1991 (xviii), Protocol of Entry into Force: United Kingdom Treaty Series, No. 2, 1966.

[14] General Assembly resolution 267 (iii).

[15] The term is used throughout this chapter to refer only to resolution A of the three Uniting for Peace resolutions adopted on 3 November 1950.

[16] The fourteen members named were Australia, Belgium, Brazil, Burma, Canada, Egypt, France, Mexico, the Philippines, Turkey, the United Kingdom, the United States, Venezuela and Yugoslavia.

[17] Vallat: *The General Assembly and the Security Council of the United Nations*, B.Y.B.I.L., 1952, p. 96.

[18] U.N.C.I.O., vol. 12, p. 503.

[19] *Ibid.*

[20] I.C.J. reports, 1962, p. 151.

[21] *Ibid*, p. 162.

[22] *Ibid*, p. 164.

[23] *Ibid*, p. 200.

[24] *Ibid*, p. 274.

[25] *Ibid*, p. 273.

[26] *Ibid*, p. 272.

[27] Wortley: *The veto and the security provisions of the charter*, B.Y.B.I.L., 1946, p. 110.

[28] Kelsen: *Recent trends in the law of the United Nations*, pp. 978–9. On the interpretation of the word 'action', Kelsen says (*loc. cit.*, pp. 964–5) that 'If the more restricted interpretation is accepted, article 11, paragraph 2, does not prohibit the General Assembly from recommending to members the use of armed force. But if the interpretation is accepted according to which action means any enforcement action whatever, the provisions of this article may be considered as constituting a restriction of the competence of the General Assembly established by article 10 to make recommendations of any kind on all questions within the scope of the charter.'

[29] Andrassy: *Uniting for peace*, A.J.I.L., pp. 563–4. In respect of peace-keeping activities generally, Sir Gerald Fitzmaurice said in his separate opinion in the *Certain Expenses* case: 'The charter does not . . . in the matter of peace-keeping activities establish any rigid general division of function between the role of the Security Council and that of the Assembly.' I.C.J. reports, 1962, p. 200.

[30] Andrassy: *Uniting for Peace*, A.J.I.L., 1950, p. 572.

[31] Sohn: *Authority of the United Nations to establish and maintain a permanent force*, A.J.I.L., 1958, p. 232. Sohn points out that part C of the Uniting for Peace resolution falls clearly within article 11 (1) of the charter and 'provides members with the opportunity to fulfil their original obligations [under article 43] through unilateral declarations rather than agreements'.

[32] Halderman: *Legal basis for United Nations armed forces*, A.J.I.L., 1962, p. 995.

Chapter III

THE MAINTENANCE OF INTERNATIONAL PEACE AND SECURITY

(2) PEACE-KEEPING OPERATIONS

AN examination of the records of the San Francisco conference discloses that the conference did not envisage any gap as existing between sections A and B of chapter VIII of the Dumbarton Oaks proposals. These sections, which were adopted with few changes as chapters VI and VII of the charter, dealt respectively with the Pacific Settlement of Disputes, and with Determination of Threats to the Peace or Acts of Aggression and Action with respect thereto. At the opening meeting of Commission III/3/1, which was charged with the examination of chapter VIII B of the proposals, the rapporteur said that the Security Council—already envisaged in the proposals as having the primary responsibility for the maintenance of international peace and security—could:

have recourse successively to all sorts of measures for the maintenance of peace, each of which reinforces the authority of the preceding one.

He then mentioned in the following order: (1) a decision by the Council to hold an enquiry, (2) an injunction by the Council to the parties to settle their dispute by peaceful means, and (3) a recommendation to the parties on the procedure which seems most appropriate. He then added:

It is after the failure of these attempts . . . or if their application seems useless from the start, that the Council has the recourse to the coercive measures contemplated in Section B.[1]

What the San Francisco conference did not envisage, and therefore did not consider, was that there might be circumstances leading to international friction or constituting a threat to international peace, or even circumstances in which a breach of the peace had already occurred, in which the Council might need to have armed forces available to it for peace-keeping operations not involving coercive measures against a particular State or States.[2]

28

United Nations forces have been established and used on five occasions during the last twenty years. With the exception of the forces established to deal with the situation in Korea—a situation corresponding to that envisaged in chapter VII of the charter, although the forces were not set up under article 43—none of these forces has been established for the purpose of coercive action, but for the more general purpose of the maintenance of international peace and security set out in article 1 (1) of the charter and with the consent of, or at the request of, the State on whose territory they have operated. My intention in this chapter is to consider the circumstances in which these United Nations forces were set up and to indicate briefly what arguments have been used for and against the legality, under the charter, of the establishment of these forces,[3] and in so doing to emphasise the gap that appears to exist between chapters VI and VII of the charter.

THE 'POLICE ACTION' IN KOREA

Although the situation in Korea corresponded to that foreseen in chapter VII of the charter, the provisions of that chapter were not, and could not, be fully applied. Therefore, although the forces established under the auspices of the United Nations were used in that instance for enforcement action and not (as were the other United Nations forces to which I shall refer in this lecture) for the general purpose of the maintenance of international peace and security, it is worth considering briefly to what extent the action taken to establish the United Nations force in Korea was based on chapter VII.

On 25 June 1950, when the representative of the Soviet Union was absent, the Security Council adopted, by nine votes with one abstention, a resolution[4] which, *inter alia*, noted 'with grave concern the armed attack upon the Republic of Korea by forces from North Korea' and determined 'that this action constitutes a breach of the peace'. Two days later, when the Council had before it a report from the United Nations Commission on Korea to the effect that the evidence pointed to a calculated attack by the North Korean authorities, the Council adopted a further resolution[5] which recommended 'that the members of the United Nations furnish such assistance to the Republic of Korea as may be necessary to repel the armed attack and to restore international peace and security in the area'. In neither of the two resolutions did the Security Council refer specifically to any particular article of the charter; but both in determining that there had been a breach of the peace and in recommending that members of the United Nations should furnish assistance to the Republic of Korea, the Security Council would appear to have been acting under article 39 of the charter.[6] This article, it will be recalled, is the first of the articles in chapter VII.

In response to the recommendation made by the Security Council in its resolution of 27 June 1950, military assistance was provided by the United States and fifteen other States. In order to co-ordinate this assistance, the Security Council adopted on 7th July 1950 a further resolution[7] which reads as follows:

The Security Council . . .

Recommends that all members providing military forces and other assistance pursuant to the aforesaid Security Council resolutions make such forces and other assistance available to a unified command under the United States;

Requests the United States to designate the commander of such forces;

Authorises the unified command at its discretion to use the United Nations flag in the course of operations against North Korean forces concurrently with the flags of the various nations participating;

Requests the United States to provide the Security Council with reports as appropriate on the course of action taken under the unified command.

This resolution, again, is not based on any specific provisions in the charter. The opinion has been expressed that, even in the absence of the special agreements for which article 43 provides, the United Nations forces in Korea could have been based on article 42 of the charter.[8] It is clear, however, that it was not so based, since article 42 envisages action *by the Security Council* with air, sea and land forces made available to it by member States, and not action by a unified command under a particular member, or particular members, of the United Nations. The authority to establish the force must, therefore, be sought elsewhere in the charter, and—although this has been questioned by Kelsen[9] and others who take a restrictive view of the interpretation of the charter—the legal basis for the United Nations forces in Korea would appear to be article 1 (1) of the charter, which specifies 'effective collective measures for the prevention and removal of threats to the peace, and for the suppression of acts of aggression or other breaches of the peace' as one of the ways of maintaining international peace and security, and does not limit such collective action to that taken in accordance with chapter VII of the charter.

As is well known, however, the Soviet Union does not accept that any action involving the use of armed forces can be taken by the Organisation except under chapter VII of the charter. On the return of its representative to the Security Council in August 1950, it lost no time in expressing this view, and thus brought to an end the unanimity which had enabled the Council to take effective action in respect of the situation in Korea. As has already been noticed in the preceding chapter, the initiative passed to the General Assembly in the face of lack of unanimity among the permanent members of the Council. 'Thus, it was by virtue of the approval of the Assembly in its resolution of 7 October 1950 that action north of the 38th parallel was continued, and it likewise fell to the Assembly to condemn the People's Republic of China as an aggressor, and to recommend an embargo against the People's Republic and the North Korean authorities.'[10]

THE UNITED NATIONS EMERGENCY FORCE (UNEF)

The first of the United Nations peace-keeping forces, as distinguished from a United Nations force intended to take coercive action, was the United Nations Emergency Force (referred to hereafter as UNEF). This force owed its origin to resolutions adopted by the General Assembly during its first emergency special session, which was held from 1–10 November 1956, and was convened under part A of the Uniting for Peace resolution.[11] The occasion, as stated in the preambular paragraphs of the first of the resolutions[12] adopted by the General Assembly, was military action against Egyptian territory by armed forces of France and the United Kingdom and 'deep penetration' by Israeli armed forces into Egyptian territory. In the first of the resolutions it adopted, the General Assembly urged as a matter of priority an immediate cease-fire. The second resolution,[13] adopted two days later, on 4 November 1956, was the genesis of UNEF. The operative part of this resolution read as follows:

The General Assembly . . .

Requests, as a matter of priority, the Secretary-General to submit to it within forty-eight hours a plan for the setting up, with the consent of the nations concerned, of an emergency international United Nations force to secure and supervise the cessation of hostilities in accordance with the terms of the preceding resolution.

At this point it should be particularly noted that what this resolution contemplates is not coercive action against States alleged to be aggressors, but action 'to secure and supervise the cessation of hostilities' by an international force set up with the consent of the States concerned.

Speedy action was taken by the Secretary-General to produce the plan called for in resolution 998 (ES-I), and on 5 November 1956 the General Assembly adopted the following resolution:[14]

The General Assembly . . .

1. *Establishes* a United Nations command for an emergency international force to secure and supervise the cessation of hostilities in accordance with all the terms of General Assembly resolution 997 (ES-I) . . .

2. *Appoints*, on an emergency basis, the Chief of Staff of the United Nations Truce Supervisory Organisation . . . as Chief of the Command;

3. *Authorises* the Chief of the Command immediately to recruit from the observer corps of the United Nations Truce Supervision Organisation a limited number of officers who shall be nationals of countries other than those having permanent membership of the Security Council, and further authorises him, in consultation with the Secretary-General, to undertake the recruitment directly from various member States other than the permanent members of the Security Council of the additional number of officers needed;

4. *Invites* the Secretary-General to take such administrative measures as may be necessary for the prompt execution of the actions envisaged in the present resolution.

In a subsequent resolution, adopted on 7 November 1956[15] at the same special emergency session, an advisory committee (with the Secretary-General as chairman) was set up 'to undertake the development of those aspects of the planning for the Force and its operation not already dealt with by the General Assembly and which do not fall within the area of the direct responsibility of the Chief of the Command'; the Secretary-General was authorised 'to issue all regulations and instructions which may be essential to the effective functioning of the Force' following consultation with the advisory committee, and 'to take all other necessary administrative and executive action'.

Consequent upon the establishment of the Force, and in accordance with resolution 1002 (ES-I), the United Kingdom and France withdrew their forces from Egyptian territory, and Israel eventually withdrew its forces between the armistice lines established by the general armistice agreement between Egypt and Israel of 24 February

1949. Despite sporadic attacks over the borders between Israel and adjoining Arab States, peace—albeit an uneasy peace—was maintained in the Middle East until the withdrawal of UNEF in 1967 at the request of the government of the United Arab Republic.[16] During this time the functions of UNEF were purely those of a peacekeeping force, and, unlike ONUC—the United Nations Force in the Congo—it was not involved in any actual fighting.

THE UNITED NATIONS FORCE IN THE CONGO (ONUC)

In contrast to UNEF, the genesis of the United Nations Force in the Congo (hereinafter referred to as ONUC) is to be found in resolutions of the Security Council. As the result of a request from the president of the newly established State of the Congo for the 'urgent dispatch of military assistance' in view of what he believed to be the possibility of Belgian intervention in the Congo, the Security Council, in its resolution of 14 July 1960[17] called upon the Belgian government 'to withdraw their troops from the territory of the Republic of the Congo', and authorised the Secretary-General 'to take the necessary steps, in consultation with the government of the Republic of the Congo, to provide the government with such military assistance as may be necessary until, through the efforts of the Congolese government with the technical assistance of the United Nations, the national security forces may be able, in the opinion of the Government, to meet fully their tasks'.

In pursuance of this resolution, the Secretary-General arranged for forces to be provided by a number of members of the United Nations, excluding (as was also the case with UNEF) forces from the permanent members of the Security Council. In his first report to the Council, the Secretary-General contemplated that ONUC would be 'built around a hard core of military units from African States' whilst 'maintaining the universal character of a United Nations operation'.[18] On 22 July 1960 the Security Council adopted a further resolution[19] commending the prompt action he had taken to carry out the Council's previous resolution.

The situation was, however, almost immediately complicated by the attempt of Katanga to secede from the newly formed Republic of the Congo, and the likelihood that it would be impossible for the United Nations force to enter Katanga without using force. Hence, the Security Council adopted, on 9 August 1960, a further resolution of which the operative part reads as follows:

The Security Council . . .

Confirms the authority given to the Secretary-General by the Security Council resolutions of 14 July and 22 July 1960 and requests him to continue to carry out the responsibility placed on him thereby;

Calls upon the government of Belgium to withdraw immediately from the province of Katanga under speedy modalities determined by the Secretary-General and to assist in every way the implementation of the Council's resolutions;

Declares that the entry of the United Nations force into the province of Katanga is necessary for the full implementation of this resolution;

Reaffirms that the United Nations force in the Congo will not be a party to or in any way intervene in or be used to influence the outcome of any internal conflict constitutional or otherwise;

Calls upon all member States, in accordance with articles 25 and 29 of the charter, to accept and carry out the decisions of the Security Council and to afford mutual assistance in carrying out measures decided upon by the Security Council.[20]

The internal dissensions in the Congo resulted in a lack of unity in the Security Council; in particular, dissatisfaction was evinced by the representative of the Soviet Union with the way in which the United Nations force, under the general direction of the Secretary-General, was carrying out its operations in the Congo. This situation in the Council led to another emergency special session of the General Assembly being convened on 17 September 1960, under the Uniting for Peace resolution.

At this emergency special session of the General Assembly, a seventeen-power draft resolution—resolution 1474 (ES-IV)—sponsored by a number of Afro-Asian delegations, was adopted without a dissenting vote. Its first two operative paragraphs read as follows:

The General Assembly . . .

1. *Fully supports* the resolutions of 14 and 22 July and 9 August 1960 of the Security Council.

2. *Requests* the Secretary-General to continue to take vigorous action in accordance with the terms of the aforesaid resolutions and to assist the Central Government of the Congo in the restoration and maintenance of law and order throughout the territory of the Republic of the Congo and to safeguard its unity, territorial integrity and political independence in the interests of international peace and security

and its penultimate paragraph was, in effect, a demand for non-intervention in the internal affairs of the Congo, and for the channelling of all aid through the United Nations. The General Assembly thus approved demands which the Secretary-General had urged on the Security Council, but which had been blocked by the Soviet Union in the Council.

Throughout the troubled situation in the Congo, first the Security Council and then the General Assembly took a hand. On 21 February 1961 the Security Council adopted a resolution [21] which urged the United Nations to 'take immediately all appropriate measures to prevent the occurrence of civil war in the Congo, including arrangements for cease-fire, the halting of all military operations, the prevention of clashes, and the use of force, if necessary, in the last resort' and which, *inter alia*, called for the withdrawal from the Congo of mercenaries and other para-military personnel, and for an investigation into the death of Mr Lumumba and his colleagues. This resolution also, however, reaffirmed the Security Council's previous resolution and the resolution adopted by the General Assembly at its fourth emergency special session.

Three resolutions adopted by the General Assembly at its resumed fifteenth session, and adopted in April 1961, [22] were also concerned to a large extent with the problem created by the presence of mercenaries and other para-military personnel in the Congo, and with the situation created by the death of Mr Lumumba. In regard to the latter, the Assembly set up a commission of investigation; it also established a commission of conciliation, with which it urged the Congolese authorities to co-operate. To that extent—but to that extent only—the Assembly inaugurated new policies.

The situation in the Congo was still complicated by the presence of foreign elements, and the danger of civil war was real and immediate. On 24 November 1961 the Security Council adopted a further resolution, the full text of which is set out at the end of this lecture. [23] Its importance is that it defines in its five preambular sub-paragraphs 'the policies and purposes of the United Nations with respect to the Congo', and that these include not only assistance to the government of the Congo in the restoration and maintenance of law and order, but also the prevention of the occurrence of civil war in the Congo; secondly, that it authorises 'the Secretary-General to take vigorous action, including the use of requisite measures of force, if necessary, for the immediate apprehension, detention pending legal action and/

35

or deportation of all foreign military and para-military personnel and political advisers not under the United Nations command', as well as mercenaries, and to take all necessary measures to prevent their re-entry or return. The resolution therefore authorised the use of a degree of force which went far beyond the limits of self-defence. It should, however, be particularly noted that the action involving the use of armed force which this resolution authorises is not coercive action of the kind contemplated in chapter VII of the charter.

THE LEGAL BASIS FOR THE UNITED NATIONS FORCES IN THE MIDDLE EAST AND THE CONGO

1. *UNEF*

The legal basis of UNEF is clearly not to be found in chapter VII of the charter. As early as the special emergency session, the representative of the Soviet Union stated that the creation of UNEF was a violation of the charter, since only the Security Council acting under chapter VII, could create an international armed force. The main arguments against the 'constitutionality' of UNEF have been summarised by Dr Bowett, in his work on United Nations armed forces,[24] as follows:

(a) that the intention of the framers of the charter was that enforcement action should only be undertaken by the Security Council in reliance on article 43 of the charter, and the special agreements referred to therein;

(b) that the field of international peace and security is outside the purview of the General Assembly, since article 24 of the charter gives 'primary responsibility' to the Security Council in such matters, and that this primacy is emphasised by article 11 (2) which requires that any question on which 'action' is required shall be referred by the General Assembly to the Security Council.

The first argument, as Dr Bowett points out, depends upon the assumption that the action undertaken in the case of UNEF was 'enforcement action' within the meaning of the charter; the second, as he also points out, contains an inherent weakness, since if primary responsibility is conferred upon one organ under the charter, this necessarily implies that there is a secondary responsibility which is vested in the General Assembly. The arguments based on the last sentence of paragraph 2 of article 11 were examined and rejected in the previous lecture in relation to the Uniting for Peace resolution.

2. *ONUC*

In the opinion of a number of authorities, the decision of the Security Council's resolution of 14 July 1960, to establish a United Nations force in the Congo, was taken under chapter VII of the charter and, more specifically, under article 40. Even if this is accepted, however, it seems undeniable that the creation of ONUC was not intended to involve enforcement action against any particular State or States, and, as Dr Bowett has pointed out, 'no specific article of chapter VII quite fits the resolutions adopted' by the Security Council.[25] This is true not only of the first of the Security Council's resolutions, which was the genesis of ONUC, but of the later resolutions adopted by the Council, including the resolution of 21 February 1961 which authorised the use of force by ONUC if this was found necessary in the last resort, and the resolution of 24 November 1961 which defined the policies and purposes of the United Nations in respect of the Congo, and included amongst them the prevention of the occurrence of civil war.

Another view, expressed by Halderman,[26] is that the substantive legal basis for ONUC rests on article 1 (1) of the charter. This rests on the assumption that there existed in the Congo a threat to international peace justifying collective measures under the charter, but it appears to be doubtful whether article 1 (1) is, taken in isolation, an entirely satisfactory basis for the establishment of United Nations forces for peace-keeping purposes.

It must be admitted, however, that it is difficult to find any other basis than the general words in article 1 (1)—the words which include among the Purposes of the United Nations 'effective collective measures for the prevention and removal of threats to the peace'— to justify the use of United Nations forces for the prevention of civil war or the arrest or expulsion of foreign mercenaries. Furthermore, if article 1 (1) is to be regarded as the constitutional basis for action of this kind, article 2 (7) of the charter, which in recent years has been too much disregarded, is necessarily relevant. This provision, it will be remembered, stipulates that 'Nothing contained in the present charter shall authorise the United Nations to intervene in matters which are essentially within the domestic jurisdiction of any State. . . .' Whilst it is also provided that 'this principle shall not prejudice the application of enforcement measures under chapter VII', it cannot, it is submitted, be disregarded if it is proposed that United Nations forces shall be used for the prevention of civil war. Such use must, at least, be preceded—as in the case of ONUC—by a request for assistance from the legitimate government, and the production of some evidence that the maintenance of *international* peace and security would be endangered by a civil war.

The opinion of the International Court of Justice

In its advisory opinion on *Certain Expenses of the United Nations*[27] the question which the Court was asked[28] to consider was whether certain expenditures which were authorised by the General Assembly to cover the costs of the United Nations operations in the Congo and of the operations of the United Nations emergency force in the Middle East constituted expenses of the Organisation within the meaning of article 17, paragraph 2, of the charter. The Court was not asked to give an opinion on 'whether the resolutions in pursuance of which the operations in the Middle East and in the Congo were undertaken were in conformity with the charter', as they would have been if a French amendment to the draft resolution had not been rejected.[29] Nevertheless, the Court did not consider that the rejection of this amendment amounted to a directive to exclude such considerations if this seemed appropriate in the context of the question actually put to the Court.[30] To that extent the advisory opinion is relevant to the question of whether the UNEF and ONUC operations were decided upon in accordance with the charter.

The Court did consider, as I have pointed out in my previous lecture, that it was necessary to examine the respective functions of the General Assembly and the Security Council in respect of the maintenance of international peace and security. After referring to article 24 of the charter, the Court pointed out that the responsibility conferred upon the Security Council by that article is primary and not exclusive. 'To this end', the Court added, 'it is the Security Council which is given a power to impose an explicit obligation of compliance if, for example, it issues an order or command to an aggressor under chapter VII. It is only the Security Council which can require enforcement by coercive action against an aggressor.' But, the Court went on to say, the charter 'makes it abundantly clear that the General Assembly is also to be concerned with international peace and security'.[31] After examining the argument based on the last sentence of the second paragraph of article 11 (which I have already referred to in my preceding lecture) and concluding that the word 'action' in that sentence referred only to coercive or enforcement action, the Court stated categorically that neither 'UNEF nor ONUC were enforcement actions within the compass of chapter VII of the charter'.[32]

As regards UNEF, the Court's conclusion is, as I have said, based to a large extent on its interpretation of article 11; ONUC was, however, established under resolutions, not of the General Assembly, but of the Security Council, and the Court's view in respect of ONUC is thus necessarily based on somewhat different considerations. The Court started with the general premise that '. . . it must be within the power of the Security Council to police a situation even though it does not resort to enforcement action against a State', and specifically in respect of ONUC said:

The operations of ONUC did not include the use of armed force against a State. . . . The armed forces which were utilised in the Congo were not authorised to take action against any State. The operations did not involve preventive enforcement measures against any State under chapter VII.[33]

In his dissenting opinion, Judge Koretsky pointed out that when the resolution establishing UNEF had been adopted by the General Assembly, the Soviet delegate had abstained and in explanation of his vote had said that he regarded 'the proposal for the establishment of an international force to be established on Egyptian territory' as 'a proposal which by-passes the Security Council and is contrary to the United Nations' charter'.[34] In respect of the operations in the Congo, Judge Koretsky's objections were not to the establishment of the United Nations force—which, it will be remembered, had been set up under Security Council resolutions—but to the fact that the General Assembly undertook those operations 'despite the provisions of the charter' and by-passing the Security Council.[35] He maintained that chapter VII of the charter 'ought to have been brought into operation when the Congo government asked for military aid to protect national territory against aggression committed by Belgian metropolitan troops'. He further considered that 'enforcement action need not necessarily be directed against a State'.[36] His arguments, in general, were directed towards an attempt to establish that the Court, unsupported by the charter, had limited the powers of the Security Council and enlarged the sphere of the General Assembly.[37]

Basing itself on the view that the only operations for the maintenance of international peace and security which can be undertaken by the United Nations are those for which chapter VII of the charter provides, and that such operations are intended to be financed by means of the special agreements provided for in article 43, the Soviet government has consistently declined to accept the advisory opinion of the International Court to the effect that the expenses of UNEF and ONUC were 'expenses of the Organisation' within the meaning of article 17, paragraph 2, of the charter. It has refused to include in the payment of its assessed contribution any element in respect of the expenses of UNEF and ONUC and, although article 19 of the charter has not been invoked in respect of the arrears so occasioned, the reasons for this are political rather than legal.

THE UNITED NATIONS FORCES IN CYPRUS (UNFICYP)

The difficulties which have arisen in respect of the financing of UNEF and ONUC have been avoided in the case of the United Nations Forces in Cyprus (hereinafter referred to as UNFICYP). This force was established by the Security Council in March 1964 in consequence of the worsening relations between the Greek and Cypriot communities in the island which led, in December 1963, to outbreaks of violence. This in its turn led to the possibility of intervention under article IV of the Treaty of Guarantee, 1960, by one or more of the three guarantor powers, and thus threatened international peace and security.[38]

The force was created under the Security Council resolution of 4 March 1964. The preamble to this resolution refers to the situation in Cyprus as one 'likely to threaten international peace and security'. The operative paragraphs relating to the creation of the Force read as follows:

The Security Council . . .
    4. *Recommends* the creation, with the consent of the government of Cyprus, of a United Nations peace-keeping force in Cyprus. The com-

position and size of the force shall be established by the Secretary-General in consultation with the governments of Cyprus, Greece, Turkey and the United Kingdom. The commander of the force shall be appointed by the Secretary-General and report to him. The Secretary-General, who shall keep the governments providing the force fully informed, shall report periodically to the Secretary-General on its operation;

5. *Recommends* that the function of the force should be, in the interest of preserving international peace and security, to use its best efforts to prevent a recurrence of fighting and, as necessary, to contribute to the maintenance and restoration of law and order and a return to normal conditions;

6. *Recommends* that the stationing of the force shall be for a period of three months, all costs pertaining to it being met, in a manner to be agreed upon by them, by the governments providing the contingents and by the government of Cyprus. The Secretary-General may also accept voluntary contributions for that purpose.

It will be noted that the force was to be established for an initial period of three months. Its mandate has, however, been renewed from time to time by the Security Council, and—not without difficulty—it has succeeded in its objective of keeping the peace. Contingents for the Force were provided initially by Austria, Canada, Finland, Sweden, Ireland and the United Kingdom,[39] and at a later stage by Denmark, Australia and New Zealand. The guiding principles relating to the operation of the Force were set out in an *aide-mémoire* by the Secretary-General. In contrast to the degree of force eventually authorised in the case of ONUC, UNFICYP is directed only to interpose itself between the two sides if this is acceptable to both. The result of this restriction is that the Force has, on various occasions, been hampered in taking action which would appear to be within the scope of its general mandate.

The other point which should be particularly noted is that, under the Security Council resolution establishing the Force, its costs are to be borne by the governments providing the various national contingents and by the government of Cyprus, except in so far as any part of these costs is met for voluntary contributions.

The legal basis for UNFICYP

The Security Council resolution of 4 March 1963 does not throw any light on what provisions of the United Nations charter the Council was acting under in establishing UNFICYP. It has been suggested that its constitutional basis is probably to be found in chapter VI of the charter, not in chapter VII, and that the creation of the Force may be based on article 36 (1).[40] This provision, it will be recalled, enables the Council at any stage of a dispute or of a situation the continuance of which is likely to endanger the maintenance of international peace and security, to recommend appropriate procedures or methods of adjustment. In the opinion of the present writer, this uncertainty as to the constitutional basis for the establishment of UNFICYP particularly emphasises the gap, referred to at the beginning of this chapter, between chapters VI and VII of the charter, and the consequent difficulty of determining what provisions of the charter, other than article 1 (1), are applicable to the establishment of United Nations forces in a situation in which there is a potential threat to international peace and security, but enforcement action is not required.

THE UNITED NATIONS TEMPORARY EXECUTIVE AUTHORITY (UNTEA)

Any description or discussion of United Nations peace-keeping forces would be incomplete without some mention of UNTEA. UNTEA is not itself a United Nations force, but a body established under General Assembly resolution 1752 (XVII) to assume for a limited time the administration of the territory of West New Guinea. This temporary administration of the territory by the United Nations was envisaged in an agreement of 15 August 1962 between the Netherlands and Indonesia concerning West New Guinea.

Resolution 1752 (XVII) authorised the Secretary-General to carry out certain tasks envisaged in the agreement. One of these was the creation and control of a United Nations security force, as envisaged in article VII of the agreement. The force so established consisted mainly of Pakistanis, but air force personnel were provided by the United States, and there were also a small number of Canadians. The establishment of the force was required because there was a potential threat to international peace and security in West New Guinea.

The constitutional basis for UNTEA

It is, again, difficult to be certain of the constitutional basis for the force. Since it was established for purposes other than enforcement action by the General Assembly, the basis cannot be chapter VII of the charter; nor can it, in the absence of any action in respect of it by the Security Council, be regarded as an appropriate procedure or method of adjustment under chapter VI. It has been suggested[41] that its legal basis is article 14 of the charter, under which the General Assembly may recommend measures 'for the peaceful adjustment of any situation . . . likely to impair . . . friendly relations among nations'.

THE SPECIAL COMMITTEE ON PEACE-KEEPING

The differences between those members of the United Nations who regard all peace-keeping activities which are not under the direct control of the Security Council as a departure from the relevant provisions of the charter, and those who consider that the General Assembly has residual powers in respect of peace-keeping, still persist; nor do they seem likely at present to be resolved by the Special Committee on Peace-keeping established on 23 May 1967 by the General Assembly at its fifth special session—resolution 2249 (S V). The wide divergences which still exist on this matter are illustrated by the debates in the Special Political Committee of the General Assembly in November and December 1967, on four draft resolutions on peace-keeping. The supporters of a nine-power resolution sponsored by Ceylon, Costa Rica, Ghana, Ireland, the Ivory Coast, Liberia, the Philippines, Togo and Upper Volta, stressed the need to ensure that the United Nations should be able to undertake peace-keeping activities, and referred specifically to the residual powers of the General Assembly in this respect. The draft resolution was, however, opposed by those who considered that it detracted from the powers of the Security Council as set out in chapter VII of the charter. On the other hand, a proposal by India, Mali, the United Arab Republic and Zambia to reactivate the Military Staff Committee provided for in chapter VII and to charge it with the preparation of a study relating to forces, services and personnel was regarded as doubtfully appropriate to the question of peace-keeping operations.

The search for some meeting of minds on the subject of peace-keeping still continues, and a working group of the Special Committee on Peace-keeping has been set up. Its members are representatives of four of the permanent members of the Security Council—France, the USSR, the United Kingdom and the USA—and representatives of four other States: Canada, Czechoslovakia, Mexico and the United Arab Republic. This working group held a series of meetings in May and June 1968, and at least agreed that a subject for study should be United Nations military observer groups established or authorised by the Security Council in pursuance of Security Council resolutions.[42]

THE CONTINUING NEED FOR UNITED NATIONS PEACE-KEEPING FORCES

In the last of his Reith lectures in 1968, Mr Lester Pearson, who has himself represented Canada at the United Nations, said that our greatest danger at the present time is that 'wars may occur, not by design, but by accident; or by conventional conflict escalating into nuclear conflict; or by a minor fight between smaller powers, each with a powerful friend whom it tries to involve in the conflict'.[43] Clearly, the need to prevent the outbreak of war, or any other armed conflict, is one of the most pressing needs of the international community. From this it follows that there will be a continuing need for United Nations peace-keeping forces, whose main function will be to keep the peace either by being stationed on the boundaries of adjacent States who might attack each other, or by being present within the boundaries of a State to prevent internecine conflict supported from outside. If the present four-power negotiations on the Middle East result in a peace plan to be put to Israel and the Arab States, it is possible that an element in that plan might be a recreated United Nations force—possibly for the purpose of patrolling a demilitarised zone.[44] Whilst it is too early to predict how this force might be set up, and what its exact functions would be, the fact that it is discussed in the press as a possibility is a reminder that it is by no means a purely academic exercise to consider to what extent United Nations peace-keeping forces have been, and can be, used to perform functions unforeseen at San Francisco and not expressly provided for in the charter.

NOTES

[1] U.N.C.I.O., vol. 12, p. 573.

[2] Bowett (*United Nations forces*, Stevens & Sons, 1961, p. 424) emphasises that situations involving peace-keeping operations must have an *international* element, and envisages a threat to or breach of international peace and security as 'the

precondition to even a peace-keeping operation'. In the view of the present writer, the presence of a peace-keeping force might be called for even in circumstances falling short of a threat to the peace if the situation were one leading to international friction, but was not an imminent threat to the peace.

[3] A much more detailed examination of the 'constitutionality' of these forces is to be found in Dr Bowett's work on United Nations forces, to which I am greatly indebted. Reference should also be made to Dr Rosalyn Higgins: *United Nations peace-keeping, 1946–1947: documents and commentary* (Oxford University Press) the first volume of which, relating to the Middle East, was published in April 1969 after the present lectures had been written.

[4] S/1501.

[5] S/1511.

[6] Seyersted: *United Nations forces*, B.Y.B.I.L., 1961, p. 362.

[7] S/1588.

[8] Seyersted, *op. cit.*, p. 439.

[9] Kelsen: *Recent trends in the law of the United Nations*.

[10] Bowett: *United Nations forces*, p. 31.

[11] Part A of the resolution, after providing for immediate consideration by the General Assembly of a case where there appears to be a threat to the peace, breach of the peace or act of aggression but the Security Council has failed to exercise its primary responsibility because of lack of unanimity of the permanent members, goes on to provide that if not in session at the time, the General Assembly may meet in emergency special session within twenty-four hours of the request therefor. 'Such emergency special session shall be called if requested by the Security Council on the vote of any seven members or by a majority of the members of the United Nations.'

[12] Resolution 997 (ES-I).

[13] Resolution 998 (ES-I).

[14] Resolution 1000 (ES-I).

[15] Resolution 1001 (ES-I).

[16] It is arguable that a United Nations force, established under a resolution of the General Assembly, cannot legally be withdrawn from the territory on which it is operating without the consent or assent of the General Assembly. UNEF was withdrawn in 1967 by the Secretary-General, at the request of the government of the United Arab Republic, without any prior authorisation by the General Assembly. It can, on the other hand, be maintained that the consent of the State on whose territory the force is operating is essential to its presence, and it would seem to have been on this basis that the Secretary-General acted.

[17] S/4387.

[18] Bowett, *United Nations forces*, p. 206.

[19] S/4405.

[20] S/4424.

[21] S/4741.

[22] Resolutions 1559 (xv); 1600 (xv); 1601 (xv).

[23] The text of this resolution—S/5002—is as follows:

'The Security Council . . .

Reaffirming the policies and purposes of the United Nations with respect to the Congo (Leopoldville) as set out in the aforesaid resolutions, namely:

(*a*) To maintain the territorial integrity and the political independence of the Congo;

(*b*) To assist the central government of the Congo in the restoration and maintenance of law and order;

(*c*) To prevent the occurrence of civil war in the Congo;

(*d*) To secure the immediate withdrawal and evacuation from the Congo of all foreign military, para-military and advisory personnel not under United Nations command, and all mercenaries; and

(*e*) To render technical assistance. . . .

1. *Strongly deprecates* the secessionist activities illegally carried out by the provincial administration of Katanga, with the aid of external sources and manned by foreign mercenaries;

2. *Further deprecates* the armed action against United Nations forces and personnel in the pursuit of such activities;

3. *Insists* that such activities shall cease forthwith, and *calls upon* all concerned to desist therefrom;

4. *Authorises* the Secretary-General to take vigorous action, including the use of requisite measures of force, if necessary, for the immediate apprehension, detention, pending legal action and/or deportation of all foreign military and paramilitary personnel and political advisers not under the United Nations command, and mercenaries . . .

5. Further *requests* the Secretary-General to take all necessary measures to prevent the entry or return of such elements under whatever guise and also of arms, equipment or other material in support of such activities;

6. *Requests* all States to refrain from the supply of arms, equipment or other material which could be used for warlike purposes, and to take the necessary measures to prevent their nationals from doing the same, and also to deny transportation and transit facilities for such supplies across their territories, except in accordance with the decisions, policies and purposes of the United Nations;

7. *Calls upon* all member States to refrain from promoting, condoning or giving support by acts of omission or commission, directly or indirectly, to activities against the United Nations often resulting in armed hostilities against the United Nations forces and personnel;

8. *Declares* that all secessionist activities against the Republic of the Congo are contrary to the *loi fondamentale* and Security Council decisions and specifically *demands* that such activities which are now taking place in Katanga shall cease forthwith;

9. *Declares* full and firm support for the central government of the Congo, and the determination to assist that government in accordance with the decisions of the United Nations to maintain law and order and national integrity, to provide technical assistance and to implement these decisions;

10. *Urges* all member States to lend their support, according to their national procedures, to the central government of the Republic of the Congo in conformity with the charter and the decisions of the United Nations;

11. *Requests* all member States to refrain from any action which may directly or indirectly impede the policies and purposes of the United Nations in the Congo and is contrary to its decisions and the general purpose of the charter.'

[24] Bowett: *United Nations forces*, pp. 95–6.

[25] A detailed discussion of the constitutional basis of the resolutions adopted is to be found at pp. 174–81 of Dr Bowett's work on United Nations forces.

[26] Halderman: *Legal basis for United Nations armed forces*, A.J.I.L., 1956, p. 971.

[27] I.C.J. reports, 1962, p. 151. By resolution 1854 (xvii) of 19 December 1962 the General Assembly, after a vote of 76–17–8, accepted the Court's opinion.

[28] The Court's advisory opinion was given in pursuance of General Assembly resolution 1731 (xvi).

[29] The amendment was rejected at the 1086th plenary meeting of the General Assembly on 20 December 1961.

[30] I.C.J. reports, 1962, p. 157.

[31] *Ibid*, p. 163.

[32] *Ibid*, p. 166.

[33] *Ibid*, p. 177.

[34] *Ibid*, p. 260.

[35] *Ibid*, p. 266; p. 268.

[36] *Ibid*, p. 274.

[37] *Ibid*, p. 272.

[38] Article IV of the Treaty of Guarantee (*United Kingdom Treaty Series*, No. 5 (1961)) states that each of the guarantor powers reserves 'the right to take action with the sole aim of re-establishing the state of affairs created by the present treaty'. During the discussions in the Security Council before the adoption of the resolution of 4 March 1964, it was suggested that this provision was inconsistent with article 2 (4) of the charter, at least as far as action involving the use of armed force was concerned.

[39] Presumably because the United Kingdom already had forces in Cyprus under the 1960 treaties and had itself made efforts to make them available to the government of Cyprus for the purpose of keeping the peace, the Secretary-General did not exclude from UNFICYP (as he did from UNEF and ONUC) contingents from the forces of one of the permanent members of the Security Council.

[40] Bowett: *United Nations forces*, p. 553.

[41] *Ibid*, p. 257.

[42] A/7201, pp. 75–6.

[43] *The Listener*, 26 December 1968.

[44] *The Times*, 9 April 1969.

Chapter IV

NON-SELF-GOVERNING TERRITORIES

THE Dumbarton Oaks proposals of 9 October 1944 (see Appendix 2) contained no provisions corresponding to chapters XI and XII of the charter, which relate respectively to non-self-governing territories and to an international trusteeship system. At the San Francisco conference it was, however, recognised that the charter of the new organisation would be incomplete if the existence of non-self-governing territories in certain regions of the world were to be ignored. The covenant of the League of Nations had itself recognised, although only in respect of 'former enemy territories', that there were certain territories 'inhabited by peoples not yet able to stand by themselves under the strenuous conditions of the modern world', and that to such territories 'there should be applied the principle that the well-being and development of such peoples form a sacred trust of civilisation'. In consequence, although only in respect of former Turkish territories and former German territories in Africa, a system of mandates was instituted by article 22 of the covenant. Under this system, the tutelage of such peoples was entrusted to certain 'advanced nations who, by reason of their resources, their experience, and their geographical position' could best undertake this responsibility. As provided in article 22, the character of the mandate differed according to the stage of the development of the people, the geographical situation of the territory, its economic conditions and other similar circumstances.

At San Francisco the committee—committee 4 of Commission II —which was charged with the task of filling the gap which was recognised to exist in the Dumbarton Oaks proposals had no terms of reference other than those in the memorandum on the organisation of the conference. These read as follows:

To prepare and recommend to Commission II, and to Commission III as necessary, draft provisions on principles and mechanism of a system of international trusteeship for such dependent territories as may by subsequent agreement be placed thereunder.[1]

It was therefore inevitable that the committee started its work by a discussion of the extent to which the trusteeship system to be established by the charter should be applicable. Should it, as suggested by the representative of the Philippines,[2] be applicable to all dependent territories, including colonies, or only to such territories as were voluntarily placed under the system?

Although it is not surprising that suggestions for the universal application of the trusteeship system to all dependent territories met with opposition, it is interesting, in the light of subsequent developments in the United Nations, to note some of the reasons given in opposing the adoption of these suggestions. The Netherlands representative considered that 'The superimposition of such a system would be a backward step from the point of view of the more advanced colonial territories'.[3] Both France and the United Kingdom considered that compulsory application of the trusteeship system to existing colonies would amount to interference in the domestic affairs of States which would be members of the new organisation.[4]

The committee did not, however, reject the concept of the development of all non-self-governing territories in the interests of their inhabitants, and side by side with proposals for a system of voluntary trusteeship put forward by the United States, Australia and the United Kingdom submitted proposals regarding non-self-governing territories. These proposals, and others submitted by China and France, together with suggestions made by other delegations, were the foundation of a working paper adopted by the committee at its fifth meeting. This working paper was divided into two sections; section A was a declaration regarding non-self-governing territories, and section B concerned an international trusteeship system. This working paper was the basis of chapters XI and XII of the charter.[5]

INDEPENDENCE AS AN OBJECTIVE

As the result of the acceptance of a Chinese amendment[6] to the proposals on trusteeship put forward by the United States, there is in article 76 of the charter—the article defining the objectives of the trusteeship system—the phrase 'progressive development towards self-government or independence'. The Declaration on Non-Self-Governing Territories—now article 73 of the charter—includes among the objectives to be pursued by administering States the development of self-government 'to take due account of the political aspirations of the peoples' in non-self-governing territories, as well as assistance 'in the progressive development of their free political institutions, according to the particular circumstances of each territory and its peoples and their varying stages of advancement'. Article 73 does not, however, refer specifically to independence as an alternative goal for non-self-governing territories.

The question of whether independence should be specified as an objective, not only for those territories placed under trusteeship, but also for all dependent territories, was discussed at some length by committee 4 of Commission II. In favour of a specific reference to independence, it was maintained that the use of this word would not imply that all dependent territories would necessarily attain independent status, but that this possibility should not be excluded by the charter.[7] Those who supported the inclusion of a reference to independence did not consider that self-government alone would be an adequate objective, particularly in view of the inclusion of 'the self-determination of peoples' among the aims of the United Nations.[8] One representative believed that independence should be conceded whenever a self-governing people had unmistakably expressed its wish for complete liberation.[9]

Arguments against a specific reference to independence were that the word 'self-government' did not exclude this possibility, but that to mention it as a goal for all dependent territories would create uncertainty which would tend to prevent capital development, and might ultimately result in the creation of numerous small States at a time when the inter-dependence of all peoples was becoming necessary and desirable.[10] Such views were summarised by the representative of the United Kingdom when he said that although 'his Government had never ruled out independence as a possible goal for dependent territories in appropriate cases', they had objected 'to putting forward independence as a universal co-equal goal for all territories'.[11] This objection, and other similar views, prevailed. A motion proposing the insertion of a reference to independence as the ultimate goal for all non-self-governing territories was withdrawn on the understanding that independence would be included amongst the objectives of the trusteeship system.[12]

When Commission II considered the report of its fourth committee the proposal made therein that the charter should contain a declaration regarding non-self-governing territories met with general acceptance. It was recognised that the declaration, although not abolishing colonialism, would put 'countries, especially colonial powers who have colonies to look after, under certain obligations, and should lead to a general improvement in administration and new ideals'.[13] The Commission, however, endorsed its committee's view that independence, although not excluded as an objective for dependent territories, should not be specifically mentioned as such in the declaration. The Netherlands delegate said that 'the realisation of self-government may take the form of a continued equal partnership . . . or that of an independent nation. That is for the inhabitants of the territory to decide.' He also forecast that 'the number of united nations at the world's conference table will grow until all people of achieving self-government will sit among us'.[14] The United Kingdom delegate on Commission II, Lord Cranborne, referred to the Declaration as codifying the principles of colonial government, and said: 'In every area, whether backward or advanced, there must be a duty on colonial powers to train and educate the indigenous people to govern themselves.'[15] He repeated that the declaration 'does not rule out independence; it leaves it to the process of natural evolution in cases where it is appropriate'. He considered, however, that to have included independence as the universal goal of colonial territories would have been both 'unrealistic and prejudicial to peace and security'.[16] This view prevailed at San Francisco, as can be seen from the text of article 73 of the charter as finally adopted.

SELF-DETERMINATION

It has already been noticed that one of the reasons why it was suggested at San Francisco that independence should be specified as a goal for all dependent territories was that the sponsoring governments had themselves proposed, as an amendment to the Dumbarton Oaks proposals, that among the Purposes of the United Nations there should be included the development of friendly relations among nations, 'based on respect for the principle of equal rights and

51

self-determination of peoples'. This proposal was adopted, and now appears as part of the second paragraph of article 1 of the charter. Article 55 of the charter also refers to 'respect for the principle of equal rights and self-determination of peoples' in a similar context.

Since it is nowadays maintained in some quarters that self-determination is not merely a moral or political concept, but is 'a natural and inalienable right which constituted one of the foundations of the United Nations',[17] it is necessary at this stage to consider what the scope of the concept of self-determination was considered to be at the San Francisco conference. It is already clear that some delegates did not consider that its application was limited to territorial adjustments in existing States; but it would seem, from certain anxieties which were expressed, that it was primarily in this context that the conference considered it. For instance, in recommending the adoption of paragraph 2 of article 1 of the charter, committee 1/1 stated that it understood

'that the principle of equal rights of peoples and that of self-determination are two complementary parts of one standard of conduct; that the respect of that principle is a basis for the development of friendly relations and is one of the measures to strengthen universal peace; that an essential element of the principle in question is a free and genuine expression of the will of the people which avoids cases of the alleged expression of the popular will such as those used for their own ends by Germany and Italy . . .'[18]

In saying this, committee 1/1 appears to have understood the concept of self-determination in the same sense as President Wilson, who, following the promulgation of his Fourteen Points said: 'Peoples and provinces are not to be bartered about from sovereignty to sovereignty as if they were chattels or pawns.' But even when the principle of self-determination was considered to be capable of a broader application, different views were expressed as to its scope: ' . . . it was strongly emphasised on the one side that this principle corresponded closely to the will and desires of peoples everywhere and should be clearly enunciated in the charter'; on the other side, it was stated that the principle conformed to the purposes of the charter only in so far as it implied the right of self-government of peoples and not the right of secession.[19]

From a study of the records of the San Francisco conference, it seems quite clear that the language used in article 1 (2) of the charter was not intended to form any basis on which a province, or other part of a sovereign independent State, could claim to secede from that State, nor to form the basis for immediate demands for independence on the part of peoples who had not yet attained a full measure of self-government.[20] If, as is now claimed, a right to self-determination for all dependent territories can be derived from the charter, it is necessary to consider whether this is expressly or impliedly recognised in chapters XI and XII of the charter.

Although the provisions of both these chapters are entirely compatible with the concept of self-determination, the expression itself is not used in either. Unless a gloss is placed on the language of article 73, it does not seem possible to derive from it any support for the thesis that it has created for the peoples of non-self-governing territories a *right* of self-determination which in the last resort would justify the use of force for its attainment. Article 73 is concerned with the obligations of member States administering non-self-governing territories, and with the objectives to be pursued by those States. Similarly, article 76 lays down 'the basic objectives of the trusteeship system. Nowhere in either of these chapters is there to be found the categoric statement which appears in General Assembly resolution 1514 (xv) (see Appendix 5) that 'all peoples have the right to self-determination'.

Can it therefore be maintained that the charter is deficient in this respect and that, as has recently been said, the 'most appropriate statement of the law of the principle' is now to be found in resolution 1514 (xv) and in the International Covenants on Human Rights?[21] Each of the latter affirms in the first paragraph of its first article that 'all peoples have the right of self-determination' and that 'By virtue of that right they freely determine their political status and freely pursue their economic, social and cultural development.'

THE IMPLEMENTATION OF CHAPTER XI OF THE CHARTER

At a very early stage, the General Assembly recognised the need to establish procedures to implement chapter XI of the charter. In a resolution adopted on 9 February 1946, the Assembly drew attention to the fact that the obligations accepted under chapter XI were 'already in full force', and requested the Secretary-General to include in his report on the work of the Organisation a summary of the information transmitted to him under article 73 (e) by members responsible for the administration of non-self-governing territories. In a resolution—66 (I)—adopted by the General Assembly on 14 December 1946, seventy-four territories were enumerated, in accordance with the declarations of the responsible governments, as falling within the scope of article 73 (e).

The determination of the General Assembly to ensure that information received under article 73 (e) was not merely summarised by the Secretary-General, but was more closely examined, is shown by its establishment, under resolution 146 (II) adopted on 3 December 1947, of a special committee composed of the members transmitting such information and an equal number of members without such responsibilities elected by the General Assembly.[22] This special committee was charged with the task not merely of examining the information transmitted, but also of submitting reports thereon for the consideration of the General Assembly,

with such procedural recommendations as it may deem fit, and with such substantive recommendations as it may deem desirable relating to functional fields generally but not with respect to individual territories.

At the third session of the General Assembly, a similar special committee with the same terms of reference was established under resolution 219 (III), adopted on 3 November 1948. The following year a similar special committee was set up under resolution 332 (IV) for a three-year period. Its terms of reference under that resolution were broadly the same as those of its predecessors, but it was specifically invited 'to examine, in the spirit of paragraphs 3 and 4 of article 1 and of article 55 of the charter, the summaries and analyses of information transmitted on economic, social and educational conditions in the non-self-governing territories', including information on measures taken in respect of such conditions in pursuance of resolutions adopted by the General Assembly.

The General Assembly, however, also adopted at its third session another resolution—334 (IV)—which, after recording the opinion 'that it is within the responsibility of the General Assembly to express its opinion on the principles which have guided or may guide the members concerned in enumerating the territories for which the obligation exists to transmit information under article 73 (e) of the charter', invited the special committee 'to examine the factors which should be taken into account in deciding whether any territory is or is not a territory whose people have not yet attained a full measure of self-government'. The language of this resolution should be carefully noted: it is entirely compatible with chapter XI of the charter and there is no suggestion that the General Assembly is purporting to create for members administering non-self-governing territories obligations additional to those specified in article 73. In deciding that it was within their competence to discuss the principles referred to above, the General Assembly would appear to have acted on the basis of article 10 of the charter, which empowers the Assembly to 'discuss any questions or any matters within the scope of the . . . charter' and to make recommendations to the members of the United Nations on any such questions or matters. Resolution 334 (IV) does not, however, refer to any particular article of the charter, other than article 73.

FACTORS INDICATING THE ATTAINMENT OF INDEPENDENCE OR SELF-GOVERNMENT

On the basis of the special committee's report, the General Assembly prepared a list of factors which should be taken into account in deciding whether a territory is or is not a territory whose people have not yet attained a full measure of self-government. This list was annexed to resolution 567 (VI) of 18 January 1952, under which an *ad hoc* committee was also appointed to continue the study of these factors. In the introduction to this annex it was stated that:

The conditions under which the provisions of chapter XI of the charter cease to apply will be that the inhabitants of the territory have attained, through political advancement, a full measure of self-government. The fulfilment of this condition may be achieved by various means, involving in all cases the free will of the people. The two principal means are (*a*) the attainment of independence and (*b*) the union of the territory on a footing of equal status with other component parts of the metropolitan or other country or its association on the same conditions with the metropolitan or other country or countries. The extent to which the provisions of article 73 (e) continue to apply in the case of territories which have become neither independent nor fully integrated within another State but which have already attained a full measure of self-government in their internal affairs is a question which merits further study.

At its next session the General Assembly examined the *ad hoc* committee's report and approved a revised list of 'factors indicative of the attainment of independence or of other separate systems of self-government' which was annexed to resolution 648 (VII) adopted by the General Assembly on 10 December 1952. This list, the resolution stated, should provisionally be taken into account by the General Assembly in examining information regarding the cessation of the transmission of information under article 73 (e) 'or in relation to other questions that may arise concerning the existence of an obligation to transmit information' under that article. The same resolution set up a new *ad hoc* committee 'to carry out a more thorough study of the factors to be taken into account in deciding whether a territory has or has not attained a full measure of self-government'. In particular, the resolution invited the *ad hoc* committee to take into account the following additional elements:

(*a*) The possibility of defining the concept of a full measure of self-government for the purposes of chapter XI of the charter.

(*b*) The features guaranteeing the principle of the self-determination of peoples in relation to chapter XI of the charter.

(*c*) The manifestation of the freely expressed will of the peoples in relation to the determination of their national and international status for the purposes of chapter XI of the charter.

This resolution, again, would appear to be entirely compatible with chapter XI of the charter. The additional elements the *ad hoc* committee were requested to take into account are all relevant to the interpretation of that chapter, and the language used does not imply concepts doubtfully consistent with, or beyond the scope of, that chapter. For instance, self-determination is referred to as a *principle* and not as a right.

At the eighth session of the General Assembly a revised list of 'factors indicative of the attainment of independence or of other separate systems of self-government', annexed to resolution 742 (VIII), was approved. This list is divided into three parts: the first lists factors indicative of the attainment of independence, and includes amongst them international responsibility; eligibility for membership of the United Nations; power to enter into direct relations of every kind with other governments and with international institutions and to negotiate, sign and ratify international instruments; the sovereign right to provide for national defence. The second part of the list enumerates 'factors indicative of the attainment of other separate systems of self-government'. Among the general factors in this case are 'the opinion of the population of the territory, freely expressed by informed and democratic processes, as to the status or change in status which they desire' and 'freedom of choosing on the basis of the right of self-determination of peoples between several possibilities, including independence'. Among the internal factors which are considered to be relevant is effective participation in the government of the territory, and the 'degree of freedom and lack of discrimination against the indigenous population of the territory in social legislation and social developments'. The third part of the list enumerates similar factors which should be regarded as indicative of 'the free association of a territory on an equal basis with the metropolitan or other country as an integral part of that country or in any other form'. A particularly noticeable factor in this case is that there should be 'citizenship without discrimination on the same basis as other inhabitants'.

It was the intention that the list of factors, as finally approved by the General Assembly, should be used 'as a guide' by the General Assembly and by the administering members in determining whether any territory, owing to changes in its constitutional status, was or was not any longer within the scope of article XI of the charter. In the operative part of the accompanying resolution, the General Assembly records its opinion that

the manner in which territories referred to in chapter XI of the charter can become fully self-governing is primarily through the attainment of independence, although it is recognised that self-government can also be achieved by association with another State or group of States if this is done freely and on the basis of absolute equality.

Although this resolution recognises that self-government is not necessarily and always equivalent to independence, there is a very noticeable change of emphasis between the views expressed by the General Assembly in November 1953, and those emphasised at San Francisco. By 1953 independence had come to be regarded as the normal and desirable goal for non-self-governing territories and, for the first time, and in contrast to resolution 648 (VII) adopted in the previous year, self-determination is referred to as a 'right' and not simply as a principle.

The next step taken by the General Assembly, in view of the different opinions, expressed as to the application of the provisions of chapter XI of the charter, was to express the opinion—in resolution 1467 (xiv)—that the Assembly should 'enumerate the principles which should guide members in determining whether or not an obligation exists to transmit the information called for in article 73 (e) of the charter', and to set up a special committee of six members, to be elected by the fourth committee, to study these principles and to report on the results of its study to the General Assembly. The special committee was duly elected, being composed of representatives of India, Mexico, Morocco the Netherlands, the United Kingdom and the United States. The committee so constituted prepared a report[23] in which it set out, in section V, part B, a number of principles. These principles were discussed by the fourth committee of the General Assembly during its fifteenth session and, as amended after discussion, were adopted by the General Assembly in plenary session as an annex to resolution 1541 (xv) on 15 December 1960.

RESOLUTION 1541 (XV) (SEE APPENDIX 4)

Since resolution 1541 has been overshadowed by the well-known resolution 1514 (xv)—the Declaration on the Granting of Independence to Colonial Countries and Peoples which the General Assembly adopted without reference to a committee—it is worth examining 1541 in some detail. After consideration by the fourth committee of the General Assembly, it was, as we have seen, adopted by the Assembly on 15 December 1960, the day after the adoption of resolution 1514. It is resolution 1541—in particular, the principles set out in the annex—and not the declaration embodied in resolution 1514 which takes into account the detailed work done at previous sessions of the General Assembly in elaborating the factors which should be taken into account in determining whether territories have ceased to be non-self-governing.

In general, the twelve principles set out in the annex to resolution 1541 (xv) are in accordance with both the letter and the spirit of chapter XI of the charter, which, the second of the principles states, 'embodies the concept of non-self-governing territories in a dynamic state of evolution and progress towards a "full measure of self-government"'. The first principle affirms that 'The authors of the charter of the United Nations had in mind that chapter XI should be applicable to territories which were then known to be of the colonial type', a statement which is fully borne out by a study of the *travaux préparatoires*. Principle I then goes on to say that 'An obligation exists to transmit information under article 73 (e) of the charter in respect of such territories whose peoples have not yet attained a full measure of self-government', and principle III states that this 'constitutes an international obligation'. Although sub-paragraphs (a), (b), (c), (d) and (e) of article 73 are couched in language suggestive of objectives to be pursued by the administering States, there seems little doubt that sub-paragraph (e) was regarded in practice not only by the General Assembly but also by administering States as a treaty obligation. The doubts and difficulties which had arisen were not in respect of the existence of the general obligation, but arose from the fact that the phrase 'territories whose peoples have not yet obtained a full measure of self-government' at the beginning of article 73 had not proved to be, in practice, a sufficiently clear or comprehensive definition of the term 'non-self-governing territories'.

On the basis of the previous study of factors, principle VI attempted to fill this gap in the charter by stating:

A non-self-governing territory can be said to have reached a full measure of self-government by:
(*a*) Emergence as a sovereign independent State;
(*b*) Free association with an independent State; or
(*c*) Integration with an independent State.

Since both 'free association' and 'integration' are phrases which, in themselves, might give rise to further difficulties, they are further defined in principles VII and VIII. 'Free association', principle VII states, 'should be the result of a free and voluntary choice by the peoples of the territory concerned, expressed through informed and democratic processes. It should be one which respects the individuality and the cultural characteristics of the territory and its peoples, and retains for the peoples of the territory which is associated with an independent State the freedom to modify the status of that territory through the expression of their will by democratic means and through constitutional processes.' Principle VII states that 'Integration with an independent State should be on the basis of complete equality between the peoples of the erstwhile non-self-governing territory and those of the independent country with which it is integrated', while principle IX stresses 'capacity to make a responsible choice through informed and democratic processes' as an essential element in integration, and states that it should be the result of 'the freely expressed wishes of the territory's people, acting with full knowledge of the change in their status, their wishes having been ascertained through informed and democratic processes, impartially conducted and based on universal adult suffrage'.

Although it is still possible to say that the principles set out in resolution 1541 (xv) are too broadly stated, and cannot without some modification apply to all types of non-self-governing territories, they have, in general, been accepted by administering States, and can be regarded as a progressive and evolutionary development of the principles and objectives laid down in chapter XI of the charter. There is no obvious conflict between the principles and the charter once it is accepted that it is consistent with the purposes of the charter to regard non-self-governing territories as being in a dynamic state of evolution.

RESOLUTION 1514 (XV) (SEE APPENDIX 5)

This resolution, it should again be emphasised, was adopted by the General Assembly in plenary session without prior reference to a committee. To quote the language of one of its preambular paragraphs, it is based on the view 'that the continued existence of colonialism prevents the development of international economic co-operation, impedes the social, cultural and economic development of dependent peoples and militates against the United Nations ideal of universal peace'. It is thus obvious that the basis of the declaration embodied in this resolution and the basis of chapter XI of the charter are different. The latter envisages the unimpeded progress of dependent territories to full self-government and does not contemplate that freedom is necessarily identical with independence. The declaration, on the other hand, proceeds on the basis that 'all peoples have an inalienable right to complete freedom, the exercise of their sovereignty and the integrity of their national territory'. Its objective, as expressed in its final preambular paragraph, is 'the necessity of bringing to a speedy and unconditional end colonialism in all its forms and manifestations'.

In considering to what extent resolution 1514 (xv) can be regarded as consistent with the charter and its purposes and hence as an acceptable element in the progressive development of the law of the United Nations, the following points are particularly relevant:

1. Nothing in the charter outlaws colonialism or makes it illegal.
2. The status of administering authorities is recognised under the charter, and the discharge of their responsibilities cannot be regarded as a violation of the principle of equal rights and self-determination of peoples. [24]

These considerations would, however, appear to have been completely ignored in resolution 1514 (xv)—in particular, in the fifth operative paragraph of the declaration which states that:

Immediate steps shall be taken, in trust and non-self-governing territories or all other territories which have not yet achieved independence, to transfer all powers to the peoples of those territories, without any conditions or reservations, in accordance with their freely expressed will and desire, without any distinction as to race, creed or colour, in order to enable them to enjoy complete independence and freedom.

Furthermore, as is stated in the third preambular paragraph:

inadequacy of political, economic, social or educational preparedness should never serve as a pretext for delaying independence.

Thus, the declaration not only envisages independence as the goal for *all* dependent territories, but in contrast to article 73 (b) of the charter, which speaks of 'progressive development of . . . free political institutions, according to the particular circumstances of each territory and its peoples and their varying stages of advancement', declares, in effect, that this goal should be achieved immediately and irrespective of the capacity of the peoples of particular territories to assume the obligations of sovereignty.

The declaration does not say in plain terms that colonialism is contrary to international law, but it does declare in its first operative paragraph that 'The subjection of peoples to alien subjugation, domination and exploitation constitutes a denial of fundamental human rights, is contrary to the charter of the United Nations and is an impediment to the promotion of world peace and co-operation.' Of course, this statement does not, in itself, conflict with chapter XI of the charter, since one of the objectives to be pursued by the administering States is said (in article 73 (a)) to be 'to ensure, with due respect for the culture of the peoples concerned, their political, economic, social, and educational advancement, their just treatment, and their protection against abuses'. But it is not consistent with chapter XI of the charter if it is understood as meaning that all types of colonialism necessarily constitute subjugation, domination and exploitation.

Although the concept of self-determination underlies the principles annexed to resolution 1541 (xv), that resolution does not specifically refer to it, and therefore leaves open the question of whether it should be regarded as a formative principle of great potency, or as a right. The declaration embodied in resolution 1514 (xv), on the other hand. states categorically in its second paragraph that 'All peoples have the right to self-determination; by virtue of that right they freely determine their political status and freely pursue their economic, social and cultural development.' As has already been seen, chapter XI of the charter does not contain the word 'self-determination'; and although it is in no way inconsistent with the principle of self-determination, nothing in that chapter—which is concerned with the obligations of administering States—can, without distortion of its meaning, be construed as conferring on the peoples of non-self-governing territories a *right* to self-determination.

If such a right exists in international law, its source cannot be looked for in article 73 of the charter. This explains, in part, why the declaration embodied in resolution 1514 (xv) is referred to in terms suggesting that it has created obligations binding on all members of the United Nations. Indeed, the last paragraph of the declaration itself states that:

All States shall observe faithfully and strictly the provisions of the charter of the United Nations, the Universal Declaration of Human Rights and the present declaration on the basis of equality, non-interference in the internal affairs of all States, and respect for the sovereign rights of all peoples and their territorial integrity.

The language of this paragraph would seem to purport to place two declarations adopted by the General Assembly of the United Nations on the same basis as the charter itself. Since it cannot be supposed that in adopting resolution 1514 (xv) the General Assembly was purporting to create treaty rights and obligations, the last paragraph of the Declaration on the Granting of Independence to Colonial Territories would seem to imply that the declaration is to be regarded as stating and affirming existing rules of international law. It is, of course, true that the General Assembly has adopted declaratory resolutions of this kind—for instance, the resolutions affirming the Nuremberg principles and the resolutions on genocide. It also adopted in 1962 a Declaration of Legal Principles governing the Activities of States in the Exploration and Use of Outer Space.[25] Such declaratory resolutions may be regarded as persuasive evidence of the existence of the rules of law they enunciate, or at least as containing formative principles of great value for the progressive development of international law—provided they are consistent with the Purposes and Principles of the charter, and that they do not contradict any of its specific provisions. Whilst unanimous agreement by the General Assembly on a statement of existing law might be 'all but conclusive evidence of such a rule',[26] a declaratory resolution, if, and to the extent to which, it contradicts the charter, does not provide such evidence, since unless and until it is amended the existing provisions of the charter must prevail. In so far as it is inconsistent with the charter the declaration cannot, in my opinion, be regarded as a re-statement or affirmation of existing law. Indeed, as was emphasised by Professor Jennings when delivering a previous series of these lectures, 'Resolution 1514 is essentially a political document.'[27]

THE SITUATION WITH REGARD TO THE IMPLEMENTATION OF THE DECLARATION

At its sixteenth session the General Assembly decided by resolution 1654 (xvi) to establish a special committee of seventeen members,[28] to be nominated by the President of the Assembly, 'to examine the application of the declaration, to make suggestions and recommendations on the progress and extent of the implementation of the declaration, and to report to the General Assembly at its seventeenth session'. On its establishment it was decided that the special committee should in future be known as the Special Committee on the Situation with regard to the Implementation of the Declaration on the Granting of Independence to Colonial Countries and Peoples. Its mandate has been renewed by resolutions adopted at later sessions of the General Assembly.[29] In 1967 the special committee held 89 meetings, and reported and made recommendations on the implementation of the declaration with respect to 48 territories.[30] Its functions were extended by resolution 2189 (XXI), adopted by the General Assembly on 13 December 1966, which requested the special committee to apprise the Security Council of developments in any territory examined by it which might threaten international peace and security. Under this resolution, the special committee transmitted to the Security Council its debates on Rhodesia, and on the Portuguese territories in Africa.[31] Another development was meetings held by the special committee in May and June 1967, away from United Nations headquarters, 'to make it easier for representatives of national liberation movements to express their views and to acquaint the committee with the progress of their struggle'.[32]

The relationship between chapter XI of the charter and the declaration regarding the Granting of Independence to Colonial Territories and Peoples, and the relationship between resolutions 1514 (xv) and 1541 (xv) (which, it will be remembered, were adopted in 1960 within one day of each other) have been the subject of prolonged discussion in relation to particular territories by the special committee, whose name is itself significant as implying that independence is the objective for *all* dependent territories. Nevertheless, the special committee has recognised in recent years that 'with regard to a large number of the small territories . . . their size and populations, as well as their geographical location and limited resources, present peculiar problems requiring special attention', though the committee still regards the provisions of the declaration as fully applicable to them.[33] It is also, perhaps, significant that in respect of such territories, in 1967 the special committee, instead of insisting on their immediate independence, requested 'the administering powers responsible for those territories to ensure that the peoples concerned are enabled, in complete freedom and in full knowledge of the possibilities open to them, in keeping with the declaration, to express their wishes without delay concerning the future of their countries'.[34]

In the view of the United Kingdom representative on the special committee, the 'question was how the interests of peoples in small territories could be served. . . . The problem to which the special committee must now direct its attention was that of countries too small, too poor or too isolated to stand alone as independent States. Not only were they unable to stand alone; often they did not wish to do so.'[35] The United Kingdom representative was not the only member of the special committee to point out that General Assembly resolutions should be regarded as 'complementary and not contradictory', and that the committee should take into account both resolution 1514 (xv) and resolution 1541 (xv).[36] The Indian representative on the committee agreed that fulfilment of resolution 1541 (xv) did not necessarily preclude the application of resolution 1514 (xv); the representative of Tanzania did not consider independence as the only expression of 'the right of self-determination' and referred, apparently with approval, to the case of the Cook Islands, whose new status was the result of an election held in the presence of United Nations observers.[37] The representative of Sierra Leone thought that 'independence of the kind that had become traditional for larger territories did not appear to be feasible' for extremely small territories.[38] The representative of Uruguay rejected the view that it was only after becoming independent that a country could decide to associate itself with another State or States, and pointed out that if this were indeed the case 'all acts of self-determination performed in various territories while they were still subject to colonial rule . . . would have to be considered null and void'.[39] Hence, several members of the committee shared the view of the United Kingdom representative that 'free association was a permissible, acceptable and duly authorised alternative to independence' and that 'the important thing was that the peoples concerned should have independence of choice'.

The views summarised above can be regarded as in no way inconsistent with chapter XI of the charter: as the representative of Sierra Leone said, in referring to that chapter, 'the touchstone of decolonisation was . . . a full measure of self-government', and the purpose of resolution 1541 (xv) was to determine whether there was an obligation to transmit information under article 73 (e). This was 'no mere technical matter, because if there was no such obligation then the territory concerned was not a non-self-governing territory under chapter XI of the charter'.[40]

It was, however, also maintained in the special committee that resolution 1514 (xv), even if it went beyond the letter of the charter, was in keeping with its spirit and 'undoubtedly had its roots in chapters XI and XII of the charter', and reflected article 55 (c) and article 1 (2).[41] At this point, difficulties begin to arise. It is the resolution, not the charter, which has to be invoked to justify certain contentions advanced in the special committee—in particular, the contention that because the resolution refers to three kinds of territories (non-self-governing territories, trust territories, and territories which have not yet attained independence) the General Assembly and its special committee can concern themselves not only with the two former, but with territories regarded by the administering States as having 'attained a full measure of self-government'; and that this is so even if the General Assembly itself has recognised the territory as fully self-governing. This is not only going beyond chapter XI of the charter, but is inconsistent with its purpose. Still more inconsistent is the view that special missions can be sent to territories which are recognised by the former administering power as now having the status of fully self-governing associated States.[42] There is, in any case, nothing in the charter which authorises the General Assembly to send visiting missions to territories which are still dependent: *a fortiori*, no such power exists in respect of territories to which chapter XI of the charter no longer applies.

RECENT VIEWS ON THE SCOPE OF THE PRINCIPLE OF SELF-DETERMINATION

Since resolution 1514 (xv) refers to the 'right to self-determination', the special committee has based some of its contentions on the existence of this right. Differing views have been expressed on the committee as to its scope and content. The representative of Venezuela stated that the term was 'to be understood in the widest sense to cover all possibilities, including absolute independence, which was the highest form of self-government'.[43] The Italian representative expressed the view that 'self-determination should, in the first place, lead to the creation of economically viable units', and that association with former administering powers should not be rejected out of hand. The representative of Iran considered that self-determination might in some circumstances serve to perpetuate a colonial situation, and gave as examples the Falkland Islands, Gibraltar and Ifni. The representative of Uruguay added, in the context of Gibraltar, that 'self-determination could in exceptional cases . . . violate the principle of the territorial integrity of States recognised in article 2 (4) of the charter'.

Although the delegate of Uruguay based his view concerning Gibraltar on the charter, other members of the special committee referred to paragraph 6 of the declaration embodied in resolution 1514 (xv). This paragraph reads as follows:

Any attempt aimed at the partial or total disruption of the national unity and the territorial integrity of a country is incompatible with the purposes and principles of the charter of the United Nations.

It was claimed that the referendum held by the United Kingdom in Gibraltar contravened this paragraph. The United Kingdom representative pointed out that the paragraph did not stand alone, and that in including it in the declaration 'its authors had been essentially concerned not with the risks of dismemberment in sovereign States, but with the possibility of dismemberment of existing non-self-governing territories or of such countries as the Democratic Republic of the Congo, which in December 1960 had barely emerged from colonial domination'.[44] The representative of Australia also understood paragraph 6 of the declaration 'to apply solely to the disruption of dependent territories'.[45] Taking this paragraph in the context in which it was adopted, this view would seem to be correct.

The divergent views on the scope and content of self-determination expressed in the special committee have recently been reflected, although stated in rather more precise legal terms, in the Special Committee on the Principles of International Law concerning Friendly Relations and Co-operation among States, which very recently—in 1968—has been considering 'the principle of equal rights and self-determination of peoples'.

The United Kingdom view of the scope of the concept of self-determination is to be found in the proposal on this principle which it has tabled in the special committee.[46] In contrast to other proposals, which state categorically that 'all peoples have the right to self-determination', the United Kingdom proposal speaks of a right to be accorded, in accordance with the principle of self-determination, by every State to peoples within its jurisdiction 'freely to determine their political status and to pursue their social, economic and cultural development without discrimination as to race, creed or colour'. This follows from the introductory statement that 'Every

67

State has the duty to respect the principle of equal rights and self-determination of peoples, and to implement it with regard to the peoples within its jurisdiction, inasmuch as the subjection of peoples to alien subjugation, domination and exploitation constitutes a denial of fundamental human rights, is contrary to the charter of the United Nations, and is an impediment to the promotion of world peace and co-operation.'[47] It will be noted that although some of this introductory statement is taken from resolution 1541 (xv), it is strictly in accordance with the charter, and that the right the proposal speaks of is a right to be conferred in accordance with the principle of self-determination. This concurs with previous views expressed by the United Kingdom[48] that 'whilst it [self-determination] is undoubtedly a formative principle of great potency, it does not appear to be capable of sufficiently exact definition in particular circumstances to amount to a legal right'.

Three of the other proposals before the special committee speak of the 'right to self-determination', and accompany this by saying in one form or another that colonialism is contrary to international law and to the charter of the United Nations.

As can be clearly seen from the proposals submitted, the special committee could not agree upon the nature of the rights involved in the principle of self-determination. Some representatives stated that self-determination 'was no longer to be considered a mere moral or political postulate, it was rather a settled principle of modern international law'.[49]

What emerged from the debate, however, was that many of those who were most insistent in claiming that self-determination is a right —an inalienable right—had doubts as to the scope of the right. In the light of the fact that the same fears were expressed at the San Francisco conference, it is both interesting and important to note that some representatives on the special committee feared that the universal application of the principle would encourage secessionist movements in sovereign, independent States. As has already been noted, the reference to self-determination in article 1(2) of the charter was not meant to imply the existence of a right of secession,[50] and at the present time a number of States, particularly newer ones, appear to consider that the principle (or, as they usually express it, the right) of self-determination should apply only to peoples under colonial rule. Others have considered that it should, at least, apply 'to peoples occupying a geographical area which, but for foreign domination, could have formed an independent and sovereign State'. The situations to which the principle applied immediately after the first world war—territorial adjustments involving the transfer of peoples to a different sovereignty—appear to have been largely lost sight of in recent years, probably because the problem facing the world today is the emergence of a number of new States and not, in general, the readjustment of boundaries between existing States.

During the final stages of the preparation of these lectures, the question of the scope and content of the principle of self-determination, and the allied question of the fragmentation of territories whose peoples have achieved independence or a full measure of self-government, have been brought into particular prominence in the context of Anguilla.

In 1927 the United Kingdom created out of some of its former colonial territories in the Caribbean the Associated State of St Kitts/Nevis/Anguilla.[51] The seat of government of these territories is in St Kitts, and as early as May 1967 the Anguillans attempted to declare themselves independent of the rule of St Kitts. The United Kingdom government, which had regulated its relationship with the Associated State by the West Indies Act, 1967, attempted unsuccessfully to reconcile the Anguillans with the government in St Kitts. In March 1969 the United Kingdom government, maintaining *inter alia* that there was a danger to the territorial integrity of the Associated State, despatched troops to occupy the island, as well as police to assist in the restoration of law and order.

The question which has arisen, and which has been discussed extensively in the British press, is whether the attempted secession of Anguilla from St Kitts was an exercise of a right of self-determination, and what should be 'the status of small islands emerging from colonial status . . . which cannot be packaged together yet cannot exist on their own without falling prey to outside powers of some sort'.[52] In the opinion of the present writer, the Anguillan situation at least illustrates the difficulty of attempting to apply uniform solutions to former colonial territories. Even resolution 1541 (xv) does not take into account fully all the difficulties which may arise, in particular the difficulty that a very small territory associated with other territories as a State may not wish the association to continue, but may be incapable, for economic or other reasons, of itself existing as an independent State.

NOTES

[1] U.N.C.I.O., vol. 10, pp. 423, 574, 607.
[2] U.N.C.I.O., vol. 10, p. 429.
[3] U.N.C.I.O., vol. 10, p. 433.
[4] U.N.C.I.O., vol. 10, pp. 433, 440.
[5] U.N.C.I.O., vol. 10, p. 607.
[6] U.N.C.I.O., vol. 10, p. 453.
[7] U.N.C.I.O., vol. 10, p. 453.
[8] U.N.C.I.O., vol. 10, p. 441. The inclusion of the reference in article 1(2) of the charter to the principle of equal rights and self-determination of peoples was the result of an amendment to the Dumbarton Oaks proposals put forward by the four sponsoring powers.
[9] U.N.C.I.O., vol. 10, p. 446.
[10] U.N.C.I.O., vol. 10, pp. 453–4.
[11] U.N.C.I.O., vol. 10, p. 562.
[12] U.N.C.I.O., vol. 10, p. 576.
[13] U.N.C.I.O., vol. 8, p. 126.
[14] U.N.C.I.O., vol. 8, pp. 129–30.
[15] U.N.C.I.O., vol. 8, pp. 156, 158.
[16] U.N.C.I.O., vol. 8, pp. 158–9.
[17] A/7429, p. 20.
[18] U.N.C.I.O., vol. 6, p. 435.
[19] U.N.C.I.O., vol. 6, p. 296.
[20] Goodrich and Hamboro: *Commentary on the charter* (revised edition), pp. 95–6; Bentwich and Martin: *Commentary on the charter*, p. 7.
[21] These views were expressed during the discussions in the sixth committee of the General Assembly in 1968 on the charter principle of equal rights and self-determination of peoples: A/7429, p. 21. The text of the International Covenants on Human Rights is to be found in Misc. No. 4 (1967), Cmnd. 3220.
[22] The members transmitting information under article 73 (3) were Australia, Belgium, Denmark, France, the Netherlands, New Zealand, the United Kingdom, the United States of America. The members elected by the General Assembly were: Brazil, China, Cuba, Egypt, India, Philippine Republic, USSR, Uruguay.
[23] A/4526.
[24] A/7326, p. 63. These two points, together with the further point that at the present time non-self-governing territories are being administered in accordance with the charter, were emphasised by certain members of the Special Committee on the Principles of International Law concerning Friendly Relations and Co-operation among States when discussing the principles of 'equal rights and self-determination of peoples'.
[25] Resolution 1962 (xviii). The principles set out in the declaration were embodied in treaty form in 1966.
[26] Sloan: *Binding force of a recommendation of the General Assembly*, B.Y.B.I.L., 1948, pp. 24–5.
[27] Jennings: The acquisition of territory in international law, Manchester University Press, p. 83.

[28] The seventeen member States originally nominated as members of the special committee were Australia, Cambodia, Ethiopia, India, Italy, Madagascar, Mali, Poland, Syria, Tanganyika, Tunisia, U.S.S.R., the United Kingdom, the United States, Uruguay, Venezuela and Yugoslavia.

[29] Resolutions 1810 (xvii); 1956 (xviii); 2105 (xx); 2189 (xxi).

[30] A/7201, p. 79.

[31] A/7201, p. 80.

[32] A/7201, p. 80.

[33] A/6700 (part I), p. 107 (paragraphs 32–3). The documents referred to under the symbol A/6700 constitute the report of the Special Committee on the Situation with regard to the Implementation of the Declaration on the Granting of Independence to Colonial Countries and Peoples, covering its work during 1967. See also A/7200, covering the committee's work in 1968.

[34] *Ibid.*

[35] A/6700/Add. 14 (part II), p. 60.

[36] A/6700/Add. 14 (part II), p. 82.

[37] A/6700/Add. 14 (part II), p. 90.

[38] A/6700/Add. 14 (part II), p. 100.

[39] A/6700/Add. 14 (part II), p. 85.

[40] A/6700/Add. 14 (part II), p. 56.

[41] A/6700/Add. 14 (part II), p. 58.

[42] A/6700, part I, p. 115.

[43] A/6700/Add. 14 (part II), p. 125.

[44] A/6700/Add. 9, p. 12.

[45] A/6700/Add. 9, p. 69.

[46] A/7326, p. 55.

[47] A/7326, p. 55.

[48] A/5725/Add. 4.

[49] A/7326, p. 59. Paragraph 3 of article 1 of each of the International Covenants on Human Rights provides that 'The States parties to the present covenant, including those having responsibility for the administration of non-self-governing and trust territories, shall promote the realisation of the right of self-determination, and shall respect that right, in conformity with the provisions of the charter of the United Nations.' If a large number of States, including at least a majority of those specifically referred to, ratify either or both of the covenants, the case for the existence of a right of self-determination as a settled principle of modern international law will be considerably strengthened.

[50] The existence of a right of self-determination is, however, invoked in this context. A very recent example of this is to be found in a letter published in *The Times* on 15 March 1969 in which the writer says: 'There is one principle at issue in the Nigerian war which seems to have so far been largely overlooked in your columns. It is the right of self-determination.'

[51] A/6700/Add. 14 (part III). In the special committee doubts were expressed, partly as a result of the absence of a referendum in the territories concerned, as to whether these territories had been fully decolonized.

[52] *The Times*, 17 March, 1969.

Chapter V

SOME RECENT DEVELOPMENTS IN THE FIELD OF ECONOMIC CO-OPERATION

DURING the discussions at the San Francisco conference on chapter IX of the Dumbarton Oaks proposals, it was said in committee II/3 that '. . . should the world again drift into the chaos of unco-ordinated national action, especially in the economic field, the maintenance of peace by even the most wisely conceived and coura-geously administered security organisation would be well nigh impossible'.[1] The conference was, therefore, very much aware of the importance of economic and social co-operation, but it was, at the same time, opposed to the inclusion in the charter itself of detailed provisions to this end.

Committee II/3 unanimously recommended—and this recom-mendation was supported during later discussions in the conference —that the Economic and Social Council, which in the Dumbarton Oaks proposals had been subordinated to the Security Council, should itself become one of the principal organs of the new organisa-tion. The charter, it was said, should not give the impression that the objectives of economic and social co-operation were in any way subordinate to the other principal objectives of the new organisa-tion.[2] In the light of later developments in the United Nations the discussions in committee II/3 on the question of which member States should be represented on the Council are of particular interest. Some representatives considered that representation on the Council should be weighted in favour of the 'industrially important countries', but the general view, which prevailed, was that no distinction should be made on this ground in considering the eligibility of member States for representation on the Council.[3] Similarly, an amendment which would have given the five major powers permanent seats on the Economic and Social Council—as in the Security Council—was rejected.[4]

In the light of the later developments which we shall be considering in this lecture, it is important to notice that it was suggested in committee II/3 that there should be a specific reference in the charter to 'the general principle of access to trade, raw materials and capital goods'.[5] The general view, however, was that 'what had already been written into the charter was broad enough to give the new organisation the necessary scope'. In supporting this view, the representative of the United Kingdom said ' . . . every attempt to say what should be done places a restrictive interpretation on the charter, and limits what will actually be done'.[6] The word 'economic' the committee, agreed, was a comprehensive one, and should be understood to include (for instance) such matters as international trade, finance, commerce, transport and 'the vast problems of reconstruction'. The charter should, however, state objectives rather than provide specific solutions for problems arising in these fields.[7] This view was generally supported, and prevailed, at later stages of the conference.

THE GENERAL PICTURE

Chapter IX of the charter, as it emerged from the San Francisco conference, is entitled 'International economic and social co-operation'. Article 60—the last article within that chapter—provides that 'Responsibility for the discharge of the functions of the organisation set forth in this chapter shall be vested in the General Assembly and, under the authority of the General Assembly, in the Economic and Social Council, which shall have for this purpose the powers set forth in chapter X.' Thus, although, in accordance with the decision taken at San Francisco, the Economic and Social Council is listed in article 7 of the charter as one of the principal organs of the United Nations, it is not autonomous to the same degree as the Security Council.

In accordance with the view which prevailed at San Francisco, the powers and functions of the Economic and Social Council are set out in broad terms in chapter X of the charter.[8] This envisages that the Council's role will be to make recommendations on matters lying within its field; to initiate action (for instance, by preparing draft conventions for submission to the General Assembly on matters falling within its competence or by calling international conferences) on such matters; and to co-ordinate the activities of international agencies dealing with such matters. In particular, one of the functions of the Council, under article 63 of the charter, is to enter into agreements with and co-ordinate the activities of the specialised agencies envisaged in article 57 of the charter. These are agencies 'established by inter-governmental agreement and having wide international responsibilities, as defined in their basic instruments, in economic, social, cultural, educational, health and related fields'.

In the wide sense in which the term 'economic' was defined in the course of the discussions at San Francisco, economic matters fall within the purview of several of the specialised agencies of the United Nations. Moreover, two of these agencies deal exclusively with monetary and financial matters. These are the International Monetary Fund and the International Bank for Reconstruction and Development. Although the United Nations Organisation itself had not then come into existence, a United Nations Monetary and Financial Conference was held at Bretton Woods in July 1944, and resulted in agreements establishing, respectively, the Fund and the Bank. Both were subsequently brought into relationship with the new Organisation under article 63 of the charter. This was not the case with the earlier Bank for International Settlements established by a convention dated 20 January 1930.

In the years following the entry into force of the charter, other bodies which are not specialised agencies of the United Nations, and which have either a regional membership or a membership which is not identical with that of the United Nations, have been set up to deal with economic matters. Some of these bodies have been established by the Economic and Social Council under article 68 of the charter; others have been created by international agreement: for example, the organisation for European Co-operation and Development (OECD) and the body known as GATT, which was established by the General Agreement on Trade and Tariffs. Also established by international agreement, but more limited in their membership, are the European Economic Community (EEC) and the European Free Trade Association (EFTA).

It is not, however, my present purpose to describe in any detail the composition, functions and powers of the specialised agencies and other organisations and bodies to which I have just referred. I have a much more limited intention: to devote the remainder of this lecture to some consideration, from the legal aspect, of three recent developments in the field of international trade and development. These are the United Nations Conference on Trade and Development (UNCTAD); the United Nations Industrial Development Organisation (UNIDO); and lastly, but of great importance to lawyers, the United Nations Commission on International Trade Law (UNCITRAL). These bodies were established not by treaty, but by resolutions adopted by the General Assembly. In each case, therefore, the constitutional basis must be sought within the framework of the charter; and it is my intention, after giving some account of the structure of these bodies and the purposes for which they were set up, to consider in each case on what provisions of the charter they are based.

THE UNITED NATIONS CONFERENCE ON TRADE AND
DEVELOPMENT (UNCTAD)

The establishment of UNCTAD as an organ of the General Assembly dates from 30 December 1964, when the Assembly adopted resolution 1995 (xix). The preamble to that resolution refers to the United Nations Conference on Trade and Development, which was held in Geneva from 23 March to 16 June 1964.[9] After recognising that the conference had 'provided a unique opportunity to make a comprehensive review of the problems of trade and of trade in relation to economic development, particularly those affecting the developing countries', and that 'Further institutional arrangements are necessary in order to continue the work initiated by the conference and to implement its recommendations and conclusions', the General Assembly established the conference as an organ of the General Assembly in accordance with detailed provisions set out in the resolution.

The members of UNCTAD are not only member States of the United Nations, but also members of the specialised agencies or of the International Atomic Energy Agency. This, in itself, is an interesting development, as it means that there is an organ of the General Assembly with a wider membership than that of the Assembly itself. There have, however, been previous examples of subsidiary bodies with functions in the economic field established by the Economic and Social Council under article 68 of the charter—for example, regional economic commissions, which have a wider membership than that of the United Nations itself. States other than members of the United Nations have participated in international conferences convened either by the General Assembly or, in accordance with article 62 (4) of the charter, by the Economic and Social Council. UNCTAD is, however, a conference with a difference, since it has a permanent organ, the Trade and Development Board, which is established under paragraph 4 of resolution 1995 (xix) 'as part of the United Nations machinery in the economic field'.

The Board consists of 55 members elected by the conference from among its membership. Twenty-two are to be from Afro-Asian States; eighteen from Western European States (including the Federal Republic of Germany) and others; nine from Latin America and Carribean States, and six from Eastern European States. The Board is empowered to 'establish such subsidiary organs as may be necessary for the effective discharge of its functions', in particular the following:

1. A committee on commodities.
2. A committee on manufactures.
3. A committee on invisibles and financing related to trade.

The Board is in general, to carry out when the conference is not in session the functions that fall within the competence of the conference. These are listed in paragraph 3 of the resolution as:

(a) To promote international trade, especially with a view to accelerating economic development, particularly trade between countries at different stages of development, between developing countries and between countries with different systems of economic and social organisation, taking into account the functions performed by existing international organisations.

(b) To formulate principles and policies on international trade and related problems of economic development.

(c) To make proposals for putting the said principles and policies into effect and to take such other steps within its competence as may be relevant to this end, having regard to differences in economic systems and stages of development.

(d) Generally, to review and facilitate the co-ordination of activities of other institutions within the United Nations system in the field of international trade and related problems of economic development, and in this regard to co-operate with the General Assembly and the Economic and Social Council with respect to the performance of their responsibilities for co-ordination under the charter of the United Nations.

(*e*) To initiate action, where appropriate, in co-operation with the competent organs of the United Nations for the negotiation and adoption of multilateral legal instruments in the field of trade, with due regard to the adequacy of existing organs of negotiation and without duplication of their activities.

(*f*) To be available as a centre for harmonising the trade and related development policies of governments and regional economic groupings in pursuance of article 1 of the charter.

The principal objectives of UNCTAD are therefore to promote a continuing discussion between developed and developing countries on all aspects of trade relations, economic aid and development. Its main emphasis has, however, been on trade 'and on the need for the integration of trade and aid policies towards the emerging nations'.[10]

UNCTAD's second conference was held, in accordance with General Assembly resolution 2206 (xxi), in New Delhi from 1 February to 29 March 1968. This conference produced no spectacular results, partly because the developing countries appeared unable to act as a united body, and partly, perhaps, because of a lack of enterprise and initiative on the part of the developed countries. Nevertheless, as the Secretary-General stated in his report on the work of the Organisation for 1967–68, all participants in the conference 'were united in the conviction, new in human history, that the world's technical progress and economic understanding, as well as its resources, made it possible to improve the material condition of the whole human race'.[11] One of the more hopeful signs was the favourable reaction of developed market economy countries to 'the strong desire of developing countries for a general preference system', and in his report the Secretary-General noted that 'agreement on such a system would help the developing countries to expand their exports and achieve the necessary diversification of their economies'.[12]

Constitutional basis of UNCTAD

In seeking the constitutional basis of the economic arrangements comprised in UNCTAD, it appears necessary to have regard to articles 1, 13 and 22 and chapters IX and X of the charter. In paragraph 3 of article 1 'international co-operation in solving international problems of an economic . . . character' is listed among the Purposes of the United Nations; and paragraph 4 states, as another of these Purposes, that the United Nations is to be 'a centre for harmonising the activities of nations in the attainment of these common ends'—that is, in the attainment of all the objectives of the Organisation as set out in article 1. Article 22 of the charter provides that 'The General Assembly may establish such subsidiary organs as it deems necessary for the performance of its functions'; and article 13, dealing more specifically with these functions, provides that the Assembly shall 'initiate studies and make recommendations' for various purposes, including the promotion of international co-operation in the economic field.

Article 13 of the charter also provides that the General Assembly has the further responsibilities, functions and powers set out in chapters IX and X of the charter. Chapter IX, in particular, gives to the General Assembly, in article 60, an overall responsibility for the discharge of the functions of the Organisation in regard to international economic and social co-operation. These include, under article 55 (b), the promotion of 'solutions of international economic, social health and related problems'. It must, however, be recognised that the charter contemplates, in article 68, the establishment by the Economic and Social Council, and not directly by the General Assembly, of commissions in the economic and social fields.

THE UNITED NATIONS INDUSTRIAL DEVELOPMENT ORGANISATION (UNIDO)

Another instance of the increasing participation of the General Assembly in the economic field has been the establishment by General Assembly resolutions 2089 (xx) and 2152 (xxi) of an autonomous organisation within the United Nations known as the United Nations Industrial Development Organisation. Its purpose, functions, structure and financial arrangements are set out in the second of these two resolutions.

The purpose of the organisation is 'to promote industrial development in accordance with article 1, paragraph 3, and articles 55 and 56 of the charter' and 'by encouraging the mobilisation of national and international resources to assist in, promote and accelerate the industrialisation of the developing countries, with particular emphasis on the manufacturing sector'. Its functions include a number of operational activities, including 'assistance, at the request of governments of developing countries, in the formulation of industrial development programmes and in the preparation of specific industrial projects. . . .' Its principal organ is the Industrial Development Board, consisting of 45 members elected by the General Assembly from among States members of the United Nations and members of the specialised agencies and of the International Atomic Energy Agency. In electing the Board, the General Assembly 'shall have due regard to the principle of equitable geographical representation', but this is not left to the discretion of the Assembly, since the resolution provides that eighteen members are to be elected from among African and Asian States; fifteen from Western European and other States, seven from Latin American States, and five from Eastern European States. The organisation is to have a permanent and full-time secretariat appointed in accordance with article 101 of the charter of the United Nations, and is to be headed by an executive director appointed by the Secretary-General of the United Nations, subject to confirmation by the General Assembly. The expenses of the organisation for administrative and research activities are to be borne by the regular budget of the United Nations. Expenses for operational activities are, however, to be met (1) from voluntary contributions by governments of States members of the United Nations or members of specialised agencies or of the International Atomic Energy Agency; (2) through participation in the United Nations' development programme; and (3) by the utilisation of the appropriate resources of the United Nations' regular programme of technical assistance. The Board reports to the General Assembly through the Economic and Social Council.

The headquarters of this new organisation are now in Vienna, and it has been put in full charge of technical assistance activities in the field of industry.[13]

Constitutional basis of UNIDO

As has been seen, the second of the two General Assembly resolutions establishing UNIDO refers more specifically than was the case with UNCTAD to the articles of the United Nations charter under which it was set up. There is, however, no reference in this resolution to article 22, which, it will be remembered, authorises the General Assembly to establish subsidiary organs. There seems indeed to be some doubt whether 'an autonomous organ within the United Nations', even although its board is required to report to the General Assembly through the Economic and Social Council, can properly be regarded as a subsidiary organ of the Assembly. In general, UNIDO has more resemblance to one of the specialised agencies of the United Nations, with the important differences that its 'charter' is to be found, not in a multilateral treaty open to members of the United Nations, but in a resolution of the General Assembly, and that the expenses of its administrative and research activities are to be borne by the regular budget of the United Nations.

THE UNITED NATIONS COMMISSION ON INTERNATIONAL TRADE LAW

Since trade is the first of the matters which were considered at San Francisco to be comprised in the term 'economic', and the General Assembly has itself recognised international trade to be the primary instrument for economic development,[14] the third of the recent developments in the field of economic co-operation, the establishment of the United Nations Commission on Trade Law, is of great importance in itself. It is also, of course, a development of particular interest to lawyers, and I now propose to consider how it came into being, what its objectives are, and what is its constitutional basis under the Charter.

The establishment of the Commission: discussions in the General Assembly

At the twentieth and twenty-first sessions of the General Assembly, the sixth committee discussed the 'progressive development of international trade', an item placed on the Assembly's agenda at the instance of Hungary.

At the conclusion of its twentieth session, the General Assembly adopted, on the recommendation of the sixth committee, a resolution —2102 (xx)—which after recalling 'that it is one of the purposes of the United Nations to be a centre for harmonising the actions of nations in the attainment of such common ends as the achievement of international co-operation in solving, *inter alia*, international economic problems' and affirming the belief of the General Assembly 'that the interests of all peoples, and particularly those of developing countries, demand the betterment of conditions favouring the extensive development of international trade', requested the Secretary-General to submit to the Assembly at its twenty-first session a comprehensive report including:

(*a*) A survey of the work in the field of unification and harmonisation of international trade.

(*b*) An analysis of the methods and approaches suitable for the unification and harmonisation of the various topics, including the question whether particular topics are suitable for regional, inter-regional or world-wide action.

(*c*) Consideration of the United Nations organs and other agencies which might be given responsibilities with a view to furthering co-operation in the development of the law of international trade and to promoting its progressive unification and development.

The report, which was called for in resolution 2102, was prepared by the Secretary-General with the assistance of Dr Clive Schmitthoff. It was sent in draft to units of the secretariat directly concerned, to UNCTAD and to the regional economic commissions established by the United Nations. Consultations were also held with United Nations specialised agencies 'and other institutions most directly concerned'.[15] In the light of his survey of the work done in this field over a number of years, the Secretary-General 'reached the conclusion that the General Assembly might wish to consider the possibility of establishing a new United Nations commission that would be responsible for furthering the progressive harmonification and unification of the law of international trade' which would work in close collaboration with UNCTAD.[16] In his report, the Secretary-General defined the law of international trade as 'the body of rules governing commercial relations of a private law nature involving different countries'.[17]

The Secretary-General's report was discussed, in some detail, by the sixth committee during the twenty-first session of the General Assembly. During these discussions, representatives of the Hague Conference on Private International Law and the International Institution for the Unification of Private Law (UNIDROIT) were present and made statements.

In general, the sixth Committee welcomed the suggestion in the Secretary-General's report that the General Assembly might establish a commission on international trade law. It was emphasised, however, that the commission should not duplicate, but should work in close harmony with, the institutions already working in the field of the development of international trade, in particular the Hague Conference and UNIDROIT. The primary purpose of the proposed commission, the United Kingdom representative suggested,[18] should be the co-ordination of the numerous activities already carried out by existing organisations and institutions concerned with the law of international trade.

Other representatives, particularly those from developing countries, while paying tribute to the excellence of the work done by the Hague Conference and UNIDROIT, pointed out, for example, that 'there was no existing organisation, either within or outside the United Nations, that was equipped to deal with international trade law on a truly wide-world basis' and that 'A commission appointed by the United Nations . . . would be able to ensure close co-operation among all United Nations bodies concerned with trade problems, particularly UNCTAD and the Economic and Social Council'. Such representatives considered that 'The task of [the] commission should be two-fold: to serve as a co-ordinating body and to formulate uniform rules of trade law'.[19] In the latter respect, it was suggested, its task would be a creative one.

Differing views were also expressed on the question, raised by the Secretary-General in his report, of whether and to what extent the proposed commission should deal with unification of conflict rules, in addition to unification of substantive rules. Some representatives shared the view of the Hungarian representative, who, whilst expressing the opinion that 'unification of substantive rules was the most effective method of reducing conflict between the laws of different States', considered that the proposed commission's work would be incomplete if it failed to deal with the unification of conflict rules.[20]

Despite the differences in the sixth committee as to the role of the proposed commission, and the scope of its activities—differences which I have thought it well to summarise, since they are reflected, as we shall see later, in the commission itself—the General Assembly unanimously adopted, on the recommendation of the committee, a resolution—2205 (xxi)—by which it decided:

to establish a United Nations Commission on International Trade Law . . . which shall have as its object the promotion of the progressive harmonisation and unification of the law of international trade, in accordance with the provisions set out in section II below.

Among the provisions set out in section II are those relating to the composition of the Commission, and the means by which it is to carry out its purposes. These are as follows:

Composition: the Commission is to consist of twenty-nine States[21] elected by the General Assembly. In electing the members of the Commission, the Assembly is to observe the following distribution of seats:

(*a*) Seven from African States.
(*b*) Five from Asian States.
(*c*) Four from Eastern European States.
(*d*) Five from Latin American States.
(*e*) Eight from Western European and other States.

In electing these members, the General Assembly is also to 'have due regard to the adequate representation of the principal economic and legal systems of the world, and of developed and developing countries'.[22]

Means: the means by which the Commission is to further the progressive harmonisation and unification of international trade are also set out in section II of resolution 2205 (XXI) and it appears desirable to quote them in full, since they reflect throughout the consensus in the Sixth Committee, endorsed by the General Assembly in plenary session, that the new Commission should co-operate with the organs and institutions already working in the field of international trade law, but should not supersede them. To this end the Commission's functions are:

(*a*) To co-ordinate the work of organisations active in this field and encourage co-operation among them.

(*b*) To promote wider participation in existing international conventions and wider acceptance of existing model and uniform laws.

(*c*) To prepare or promote the adoption of new international conventions, model laws and uniform laws and promote the codification and wider acceptance of international trade terms, provisions, customs and practices, in collaboration, where appropriate, with the organizations operating in this field.

(*d*) To promote ways and means of ensuring a uniform interpretation and application of international conventions and uniform laws in the field of the law of international trade.

(*e*) To collect and disseminate information on national legislation and modern legal developments, including case law, in the field of the law of international trade.

(*f*) To establish and maintain a close collaboration with UNCTAD.

(*g*) To maintain liaison with other United Nations organs and specialised agencies concerned with international trade.

The newly established United Nations Commission on International Trade Law (UNCITRAL) held its first session at United Nations headquarters in New York from 29 January to 26 February 1968, and submitted its report on this session[23] simultaneously to the General Assembly and to UNCTAD. At this first session, all the States members of the Commission were represented; and in addition there were observers from UNCTAD, and from four of the specialised agencies, as well as observers from non-governmental organisations, including the Hague Conference and UNIDROIT. The Commission decided that every effort should be made to reach its decisions by way of consensus.

During the general debate in the Commission, there was discussion of the definition in the Secretary-General's report of 'the law of international trade', to which I have already drawn attention, and which, it will be recalled, defined it as 'the body of rules governing commercial relations of a private law nature involving different countries'. Some delegates thought that this definition was not sufficiently wide, and that questions of public international law should also be included. No decision was, however, taken by the Commission at its first session to substitute for this definition a wider one.

The general debate was followed by a more detailed discussion on such matters as the collection and dissemination of information concerning trade law, and the topics to be considered by the Commission. In considering its future programme of work, the Commission decided[24] that priority should be given to the following topics:

1. International sale of goods;[25]
2. International payments, including under this heading (a) negotiable instruments and bankers' commercial credits, and (b) guarantees and securities;
3. Commercial arbitration;

and that work on these three topics might proceed concurrently. A working group consisting of fourteen of the member States was set up to decide on methods of work for the priority topics,[26] and its recommendations were approved by the Commission at its twenty-first meeting on 23 February 1968.

During its general debate at its first session, the newly established Commission heard the hope expressed that 'out of the co-operative endeavours of the Commission and of other bodies active in the field, a new *lex mercatoria* would in time evolve, reflecting the interests of the whole international community'.[27]

Constitutional basis of UNCITRAL

The establishment of the Commission is itself an evolutionary development, and it is interesting to note that the General Assembly, when setting it up, expressed in the preamble to resolution 2205 (XXI) a definite view as to its constitutional basis. After reciting its conviction that it would 'be desirable for the United Nations to play a more active role towards reducing or removing legal obstacles to the flow of international trade', the General Assembly noted 'that such action would be properly within the scope and competence of the Organisation under the terms of article 1, paragraph 3, and article 3, and of chapters IX and X of the charter of the United Nations' and, after recognising 'that there is no existing United Nations organ which is both familiar with this technical legal subject and able to devote sufficient time to work in this field', decided to establish a United Nations Commission on International Trade Law.

CONCLUSION

The developments in the economic field summarised in this chapter are all of great importance to the evolution of the law of the United Nations. None of them would seem to be contrary to the charter; unless an extremely restrictive view is taken of the interpretation of the charter, and it is considered that the Organisation can do only what is specifically provided for therein, none of them would seem to be open to question on legal grounds. Indeed, it would seem to be difficult to raise any objection in view of the intention, clearly expressed at San Francisco, that the charter should state objectives, rather than provide specific solutions, in the economic field. So far as the United Nations Commission on International Trade Law is concerned, it is not simply the establishment of the Commission which is a stage in the evolution of international law. The Commission itself will have an important part to play in the progressive development of international law and its codification in the field of international trade, as well as of its unification. In this context I may, perhaps, be allowed to end by quoting my own father. At the end of his work on comparative law he said:

The most urgent problem of all, however, is that of the waste of effort and confusion that has, at times, been caused by the existence of competing agencies engaged in the work of unification. The remedy for this state of affairs would seem to lie in the establishment of a rallying ground for unificatory activities—a kind of international clearing house—which would co-ordinate and supervise activities of this nature and also facilitate the collection of any information that might be required, either from governmental or other sources.

The exercise of these co-ordinating and supervisory functions would appear to be a task falling within the province of the Economic and Social Council established under the provisions of the charter of the United Nations. It is, in any event, certain that the solution of most of the problems which at present, render the unification of law in the international sphere a matter of great difficulty can only be reached by the provision of some means by which the movement may be guided in the proper channels, so that the law may be unified in the directions in which uniformity is both necessary and practicable.[28]

The establishment of the United Nations Commission on International Trade Law would seem to meet the necessity my father foresaw, and I am certain that he would have welcomed it.

NOTES

[1] U.N.C.I.O., vol. 10, p. 279.
[2] U.N.C.I.O., vol. 10, pp. 17, 229.
[3] U.N.C.I.O., vol. 10, p. 53.
[4] U.N.C.I.O., vol. 10, p. 277.
[5] U.N.C.I.O., vol. 10, p. 129. The committee also agreed (*ibid*, p. 273) that the charter should not include provisions for the creation of a specialised organisation to deal with problems relating to raw materials or with cognate problems relating to capital goods.
[6] U.N.C.I.O., vol. 10, pp. 141–2.
[7] U.N.C.I.O., vol. 10, p. 230.
[8] As mentioned in Chapter I, the membership of the Economic and Social Council was increased from eighteen to twenty-seven as the result of an amendment to article 61 of the charter which entered into force on 31 August 1965.
[9] A decision to convene the conference was taken by the Economic and Social Council in its resolution 917 (xxiv) of 3 August 1962 and was endorsed by the General Assembly on 8 December 1962 by the adoption of resolution 1785 (xvii) which recalled a previous resolution—1707 (xvi)—entitled 'International trade as the primary instrument for economic development'. In adopting its resolution convening the conference, the Economic and Social Council recognised 'the importance of increasing the ... inflow of long-term capital to developed countries', but the thrust of the resolution was 'the vital importance of the

rapid growth of exports and export earnings of developing countries' and 'of primary products for promoting their economic development'. Metzger: *Developments in the law and institutions of international economic relations*, UNCTAD, *A.J.I.L.*, 1967, p. 758.

[10] *The Observer*, 20 May 1968.

[11] A/7201, p. 155.

[12] A/7201, p. 155.

[13] A/7201, p. 165.

[14] Resolution 1707 (XVI).

[15] A/C6/SR 946.

[16] The Secretary-General's report is contained in full in document A/6396.

[17] A/6396, paragraph 10.

[18] A/C6/SR 949, paragraph 11.

[19] A/C6/SR 949, paragraph 10.

[20] A/C6/SR 946, paragraph 8.

[21] The decision that the members of the commission should be States can be contrasted with the General Assembly's earlier decision on membership of the International Law Commission. The members of that commission are 'persons of recognised competence in international law' elected by the General Assembly from a list of candidates nominated by the governments of member States of the United Nations. (Statute of the International Law Commission annexed to General Assembly resolution 174(II).)

[22] The States which are members of the commission are Argentina, Australia, Belgium, Brazil, Chile, Colombia, Congo (Democratic Republic), Czechoslovakia, France, Ghana, Hungary, India, Iran, Italy, Japan, Kenya, Mexico, Nigeria, Norway, Rumania, Spain, Syria, Thailand, Tunisia, the USSR, the UAR, the United Kingdom, the United Republic of Tanzania and the USA.

[23] A/7216. See also A/7408, report of the sixth committee of the General Assembly, for a summary of the work of UNCITRAL during its first session.

[24] A/7216, p. 7.

[25] It was agreed that under this heading special attention should be given to the Hague Convention, 1964; to the Hague Convention on Applicable Law, 1955; to time limits and, in general, limitation; and to general conditions of sale.

[26] A/7216, p. 13.

[27] A/7216, p. 7.

[28] Gutteridge: *Comparative law*, pp. 184–5.

Appendix 1

PREAMBLE, PURPOSES AND PRINCIPLES OF THE UNITED NATIONS' CHARTER

I. THE PREAMBLE

We, the peoples of the United Nations, determined

to save succeeding generations from the scourge of war, which twice in our lifetime has brought untold sorrow to mankind, and

to reaffirm faith in fundamental human rights, in the dignity and worth of the human person, in the equal rights of men and women and of nations large and small, and

to establish conditions under which justice and respect for the obligations arising from treaties and other sources of international law can be maintained, and

to promote social progress and better standards of life in larger freedom,

and for these ends

to practice tolerance and live together in peace with one another as good neighbors, and

to unite our strength to maintain international peace and security, and

to ensure, by the acceptance of principles and the institution of methods, that armed force shall not be used, save in the common interest, and

to employ international machinery for the promotion of the economic and social advancement of all peoples,

have resolved to combine our efforts to accomplish these aims.

Accordingly, our respective governments, through representatives assembled in the city of San Francisco, who have exhibited their full powers found to be in good and due form, have agreed to the present charter of the United Nations and do hereby establish an international organisation to be known as the United Nations.

II. PURPOSES AND PRINCIPLES (CHAPTER I)

Article 1

The Purposes of the United Nations are:

1. To maintain international peace and security, and to that end: to take effective collective measures for the prevention and removal of threats to the peace, and for the suppression of acts of aggression or other breaches of the peace, and to bring about by peaceful means, and in conformity with the principles of justice and international law, adjustment or settlement of international disputes or situations which might lead to a breach of the peace;

APPENDIX 1

2. To develop friendly relations among nations, based on respect for the principle of equal rights and self-determination of peoples, and to take other appropriate measures to strengthen universal peace;

3. To achieve international co-operation in solving international problems of an economic, social, cultural, or humanitarian character, and in promoting and encouraging respect for human rights and for fundamental freedoms for all without distinction as to race, sex, language or religion; and

4. To be a centre for harmonising the actions of nations in the attainment of these common ends.

Article 2

The Organisation and its members, in pursuit of the Purposes stated in article 1, shall act in accordance with the following Principles:

1. The Organisation is based on the principle of the sovereign equality of all its members.

2. All members, in order to ensure to all of them the rights and benefits resulting from membership, shall fulfil in good faith the obligations assumed by them in accordance with the present charter.

3. All members shall settle their international disputes by peaceful means in such a manner that international peace and security, and justice, are not endangered.

4. All members shall refrain in their international relations from the threat or use of force against the territorial integrity or political independence of any State, or in any other manner inconsistent with the Purposes of the United Nations.

5. All members shall give the United Nations every assistance in any action it takes in accordance with the present charter, and shall refrain from giving assistance to any State against which the United Nations is taking preventive or enforcement action.

6. The Organisation shall ensure that states which are not members of the United Nations act in accordance with these Principles so far as may be necessary for the maintenance of international peace and security.

7. Nothing contained in the present charter shall authorise the United Nations to intervene in matters which are essentially within the domestic jurisdiction of any State or shall require the members to submit such matters to settlement under the present charter; but this principle shall not prejudice the application of enforcement measures under chapter VII.

Appendix 2

THE DUMBARTON OAKS PROPOSALS
9 October 1944

Agreement was reached on a wide range of subjects, and tentative proposals have been made for the establishment of a general international organisation under the title of The United Nations.

The proposals, which are set out in full below, deal with the purposes, principles, and membership of the organisation, its principal organs, including a General Assembly, a Security Council, and an International Court of Justice; the composition, functions, and powers of the General Assembly and the Security Council; arrangements for the maintenance of international peace and security; international economic and social co-operation; and transitional arrangements.

The British, United States, Russian, and Chinese governments have agreed that after further study of the tentative proposals now published they will as soon as possible take the necessary steps with a view to the preparation of complete proposals which could then serve as a basis of discussion at a full conference of the United Nations.

The full report of the tentative proposals is as follows:

There should be established an international organisation under the title of The United Nations, the charter of which should contain provisions necessary to give effect to the proposals which follow:

CHAPTER I. PURPOSES

The purposes of the organisation should be: (1) to maintain international peace and security; and to that end to take effective collective measures for the prevention and removal of threats to the peace and the suppression of acts of aggression or other breaches of the peace, and to bring about by peaceful means the adjustment or settlement of international disputes which may lead to a breach of the peace; (2) to develop friendly relations among nations and to take other appropriate measures to strengthen universal peace; (3) to achieve international co-operation in the solution of international economic, social, and other humanitarian problems; and (4) to afford a centre for harmonising the actions of nations in the achievement of these common ends.

CHAPTER II. PRINCIPLES

In pursuit of the purposes mentioned in chapter I the organisation and its members should act in accordance with the following principles:

(1) The organisation is based on the principle of the sovereign equality of all peace-loving States.

(2) All members of the organisation undertake, in order to ensure to all of them the rights and benefits resulting from membership in the organisa-

tion, to fulfil the obligations assumed by them in accordance with the charter.

(3) All members of the organisation shall settle their disputes by peaceful means in such a manner that international peace and security are not endangered.

(4) All members of the organisation shall refrain in their international relations from the threat or use of force in any manner inconsistent with the purposes of the organisation.

(5) All members of the organisation shall give every assistance to the organisation in any action undertaken by it in accordance with the provisions of the charter.

(6) All members of the organisation shall refrain from giving assistance to any State against which preventive or enforcement action is being undertaken by the organisation.

The organisation should ensure that States not members of the organisation act in accordance with these principles so far as may be necessary for the maintenance of international peace and security.

CHAPTER III. MEMBERSHIP

Membership of the organisation should be open to all peace-loving States.

CHAPTER IV. PRINCIPAL ORGANS

(1) The organisation should have as its principal organs: (*a*) a General Assembly; (*b*) a Security Council; (*c*) an International Court of Justice; and (*d*) a secretariat.

(2) The organisation should have such subsidiary agencies as may be found necessary.

CHAPTER V. THE GENERAL ASSEMBLY

(*A*) *Composition*

All members of the organisation should be members of the General Assembly and should have a number of representatives to be specified in the charter.

(*B*) *Functions and powers*

(1) The General Assembly should have the right to consider the general principles of co-operation in the maintenance of international peace and security, including the principles governing disarmament and the regulation of armaments; to discuss any questions relating to the maintenance of international peace and security brought before it by any member or members of the organisation or by the Security Council; and to make recommendations with regard to any such principles or questions. Any such questions on which action is necessary should be referred to the Security Council by the General Assembly either before or after discussion. The General Assembly should not on its own initiative make recommendations on any matter relating to the maintenance of international peace and security which is being dealt with by the Security Council.

(2) The General Assembly should be empowered to admit new members to the organisation upon the recommendation of the Security Council.

(3) The General Assembly should, on the recommendations of the Security Council, be empowered to suspend from the exercise of any rights or privileges of membership any member of the organisation against which preventive or enforcement action shall have been taken by the Security Council. The exercise of the rights and privileges thus suspended may be restored by the decision of the Security Council. The General Assembly should be empowered on the recommendation of the Security Council to expel from the organisation any member of the organisation which persistently violates the principles contained in the charter.

(4) The General Assembly should elect the non-permanent members of the Security Council and the members of the Economic and Social Council provided for in chapter IX. It should be empowered to elect, on the recommendation of the Security Council, the secretary-general of the organisation. It should perform such functions in relation to the election of the judges of the International Court of Justice as may be conferred upon it by the statute of the Court.

(5) The General Assembly should apportion the expenses among the members of the organisation, and should be empowered to approve the budgets of the organisation.

(6) The General Assembly should initiate studies and make recommendations for the purpose of promoting international co-operation in political, economic and social fields and of adjusting situations likely to impair the general welfare.

(7) The General Assembly should make recommendations for the co-ordination of the policies of international economic, social, and other specialised agencies brought into relation with the organisation in accordance with agreements between such agencies and the organisation.

(8) The General Assembly should receive and consider annual and special reports from the security Council and reports from other bodies of the organisation.

(C) Voting

(1) Each member of the organisation should have one vote in the General Assembly.

(2) Important decisions of the General Assembly, including recommendations with respect to the maintenance of international peace and security; the election of members of the Security Council; the election of members of the Economic and Social Council; the admission of members, suspension of exercise of the rights and privileges of members, and the expulsion of members; and budgetary questions should be made by a two-thirds majority of those present and voting. On other questions, including the determination of additional categories of questions to be decided by a two-thirds majority, the decisions of the General Assembly should be made by a simple majority vote.

(D) Procedure

(1) The General Assembly should meet in regular annual sessions and in such special sessions as occasion may require.

(2) The General Assembly should adopt its own rules of procedure and elect its president for each session.

(3) The General Assembly should be empowered to set up such bodies and agencies as it may deem necessary for the performance of its functions.

CHAPTER VI. THE SECURITY COUNCIL

(A) Composition

The Security Council should consist of one representative of each of eleven members of the organisation. Representatives of the United States, the United Kingdom of Great Britain and Northern Ireland, the Union of Soviet Socialist Republics, the Republic of China and, in due course, France should have permanent seats. The General Assembly should elect six States to fill the non-permanent seats. These six States should be elected for a term of two years, three retiring each year. They should not be immediately eligible for re-election. In the first election of the non-permanent members three should be chosen by the General Assembly for one-year terms and three for two-year terms.

(B) Principal functions and powers

(1) In order to ensure prompt and effective action by the organisation, members of the organisation should by the charter confer on the Security Council primary responsibility for the maintenance of international peace and security and should agree that in carrying out these duties under this responsibility it should act on their behalf.

(2) In discharging these duties the Security Council should act in accordance with the purposes and principles of the organisation.

(3) The specific powers conferred on the Security Council in order to carry out these duties are laid down in chapter VIII.

(4) All members of the organisation should obligate themselves to accept the decisions of the Security Council and to carry them out in accordance with the provisions of the charter.

(5) In order to promote the establishment and maintenance of international peace and security with the least diversion of the world's human and economic resources for armament the Security Council with the assistance of the military staff committee referred to in chapter VIII, section (B), paragraph 9, should have the responsibility for formulating plans for the establishment of a system of regulations of armaments for submission to the members of the organisation.

(C) Voting

(Note.—The question of voting procedure in the Security Council is still under consideration.)

(D) Procedure

(1) The Security Council should be so organised as to be able to function continuously and each State member of the Security Council should be permanently represented at the headquarters of the organisation. It may hold meetings at such other places as in its judgment may best facilitate its

work. There should be periodic meetings at which each State member of the Security Council could, if it so desired, be represented by any member of the government or some other special representative.

(2) The Security Council should be empowered to set up such bodies or agencies as it may deem necessary for the performance of its functions, including regional sub-committees of the military staff committee.

(3) The Security Council should adopt its own rules of procedure, including the method of selecting its president.

(4) Any member of the organisation should participate in the discussion of any question brought before the Security Council whenever the Security Council considers that the interests of that member of the organisation are especially affected.

(5) Any member of the organisation not having a seat on the Security Council and any State not a member of the organisation if it is a party to a dispute under consideration by the Security Council should be invited to participate in the discussion relating to the dispute.

CHAPTER VII. AN INTERNATIONAL COURT OF JUSTICE

(1) There should be an International Court of Justice which should constitute the principal judicial organ of the organisation.

(2) The Court should be constituted and should function in accordance with a statute which should be annexed to and be a part of the charter of the organisation.

(3) The statute of the Court of International Justice should be either (*a*) the statute of the Permanent Court of International Justice, continued in force with such modifications as may be desirable, or (*b*) a new statute in the preparation of which the statute of the Permanent Court of International Justice should be used as a basis.

(4) All members of the organisation should, *ipso facto*, be parties to the statute of the International Court of Justice.

(5) Conditions under which States not members of the organisation may become parties to the statute of the International Court of Justice should be determined in each case by the General Assembly upon the recommendation of the Security Council.

CHAPTER VIII. INTERNATIONAL PEACE AND SECURITY

(*A*) *The pacific settlement of disputes*

(1) The Security Council should be empowered to investigate any dispute, or any situation which may lead to international friction or give rise to a dispute, in order to determine whether its continuance is likely to endanger the maintenance of international peace and security.

(2) Any State, whether a member of the organisation or not, may bring any such dispute or situation to the attention of the General Assembly or of the Security Council.

(3) The parties to any dispute the continuance of which is likely to endanger the maintenance of international peace and security should obligate themselves, first of all, to seek a solution by negotiation, mediation, conciliation, arbitration, or judicial settlement, or other peaceful

means of their own choice. The Security Council should call upon the parties to settle their dispute by such means.

(4) If, nevertheless, parties to a dispute of the nature referred to in paragraph 3 fail to settle it by the means indicated in that paragraph, they should obligate themselves to refer it to the Security Council. The Security Council should in each case decide whether or not the continuance of the particular dispute is in fact likely to endanger the maintenance of international peace and security and, accordingly, whether the Security Council should deal with the dispute and, if so, whether it should take action under paragraph 5.

(5) The Security Council should be empowered at any stage of a dispute of the nature referred to in paragraph 3 to recommend appropriate procedures or methods of adjustments.

(6) Justiciable disputes should normally be referred to the International Court of Justice. The Security Council should be empowered to refer to the Court for advice on legal questions connected with other disputes.

(7) The provisions of paragraphs 1–6 of section VIII (A) should not apply to situations or disputes arising out of matters which by international law are solely within the domestic jurisdiction of the State concerned.

(B) Determination of threats to the peace or acts of aggression, and action with respect thereto

(1) Should the Security Council deem that a failure to settle a dispute in accordance with the procedures indicated in paragraph 3 of section A, or in accordance with its recommendations made under paragraph (5) of section (A), constitutes a threat to the maintenance of international peace and security, it should take any measures necessary for the maintenance of international peace and security in accordance with the purposes and principles of the organisation.

(2) In general, the Security Council should determine the existence of any threat to the peace, breach of the peace or act of aggression and should make recommendations or decide upon measures to be taken to maintain or restore peace and security.

(3) The Security Council should be empowered to determine what diplomatic, economic, or other measures not involving the use of armed force should be employed to give effect to its decisions, and to call upon members of the organisation to apply such measures. Such measures may include complete or partial interruption of rail, sea, air, postal, telegraphic, radio, and other means of communication, and the severance of diplomatic and economic relations.

(4) Should the Security Council consider such measures to be inadequate, it should be empowered to take such action by air, naval, or land forces as may be necessary to maintain or restore international peace and security. Such action may include demonstrations, blockade, and other operations by air, sea, or land forces of members of the organisation.

(5) In order that all members of the organisation should contribute to the maintenance of international peace and security, they should undertake

to make available to the Security Council, on its call and in accordance with a special agreement or agreements concluded among themselves, armed forces, facilities, and assistance necessary for the purpose of maintaining international peace and security. Such agreement or agreements should govern the numbers and types of forces and the nature of the facilities and assistance to be provided. The special agreement or agreements should be negotiated as soon as possible, and should in each case be subject to approval by the Security Council and to ratification by the signatory States in accordance with their constitutional processes.

(6) In order to enable urgent military measures to be taken by the organisation, there should be held immediately available by the members of the organisation national air force contingents for combined international enforcement action. The strength and degree of readiness of these contingents and plans for their combined action should be determined by the Security Council, with the assistance of the military staff committee, within the limits laid down in the special agreement or agreements referred to in paragraph (5).

(7) The action required to carry out the decisions of the Security Council for the maintenance of international peace and security should be taken by all members of the organisation in co-operation, or by some of them, as the Security Council may determine. This undertaking should be carried out by the members of the organisation by their own action and through action of the appropriate specialised organisations and agencies of which they are members.

(8) Plans for the application of armed force should be made by the Security Council with the assistance of the military staff committee referred to in paragraph (9).

(9) There should be established a military staff committee, the functions of which should be to advise and assist the Security Council on all questions relating to the Security Council's military requirements for the maintenance of international peace and security, to the employment and command of forces placed at its disposal, to the regulation of armaments and to possible disarmament. It should be responsible under the Security Council for the strategic direction of any armed forces placed at the disposal of the Security Council. The committee should be composed of the chiefs of staff of the permanent members of the Security Council or their representatives. Any member of the organisation not permanently represented on the committee should be invited by the committee to be associated with it when the efficient discharge of the committee's responsibilities requires that such a State should participate in its work. Questions of command of forces should be worked out subsequently.

(10) The members of the organisation should join in affording mutual assistance in carrying out the measures decided upon by the Security Council.

(11) Any State, whether a member of the organisation or not, which finds itself confronted with special economic problems arising from the carrying out of measures which have been decided upon by the Security Council should have the right to consult the Security Council in regard to a solution of these problems.

(C) Regional arrangements

(1) Nothing in the charter should preclude the existence of regional arrangements or agencies for dealing with such matters relating to the maintenance of international peace and security as are appropriate for regional action, provided such arrangements or agencies and their activities are consistent with the purposes and principles of the organisation. The Security Council should encourage settlement of local disputes through such regional arrangements or by such regional agencies either on the initiative of the States concerned or by reference from the Security Council.

(2) The Security Council should, where appropriate, utilise such arrangements or agencies for enforcement action under its authority but no enforcement action should be taken under regional arrangements or by regional agencies without the authorisation of the Security Council.

(3) The Security Council should at all times be kept fully informed of activities undertaken or in contemplation under regional arrangements or by regional agencies for the maintenance of international peace and security.

CHAPTER IX. INTERNATIONAL ECONOMIC AND SOCIAL CO-OPERATION

(A) Purpose and relationship

(1) With a view to the creation of conditions of stability and well-being which are necessary for peaceful and friendly relations among nations, the organisation should facilitate solutions of international economic, social, and other humanitarian problems, and promote respect for human rights and fundamental freedoms. Responsibility for the discharge of this function should be vested in the General Assembly and under the authority of the General Assembly in an Economic and Social Council.

(2) The various specialised economic, social, and other organisations and agencies would have responsibilities in their respective fields as defined in their statutes. Each such organisation or agency should be brought into relationship with the organisation on terms to be determined by agreement between the Economic and Social Council and the appropriate authorities of the specialised organisation or agency, subject to approval by the General Assembly.

(B) Composition and voting

The Economic and Social Council should consist of representatives of eighteen members of the organisation. The States to be represented for this purpose should be elected by the General Assembly for terms of three years. Each such State should have one representative, who should have one vote. Decisions of the Economic and Social Council should be taken by simple majority vote of those present and voting.

(C) Functions and powers of the Economic and Social Council

The Economic and Social Council should be empowered: (a) to carry out, within the scope of its functions, recommendations of the General Assembly; (b) to make recommendations on its own initiative with respect to international, economic, social, and other humanitarian matters; (c) to receive and consider reports from the economic, social, and other organisations or agencies brought into relationship with the organisation, and to co-ordinate their activities through consultations with, and recommendations to such organisations or agencies; (d) to examine the administrative budgets of such specialised organisations or agencies with a view to making recommendations to the organisation or agencies concerned; (e) to enable the secretary-general to provide information to the Security Council; (f) to assist the Security Council upon its request; and (g) to perform such other functions within the general scope of its competence as may be assigned to it by the General Assembly.

(D) Organisation and procedure

(1) The Economic and Social Council should set up an economic commission, a social commission, and such other commissions as may be required. These commissions should consist of experts. There should be a permanent staff which should constitute a part of the secretariat of the organisation.

(2) The Economic and Social Council should make suitable arrangements for representatives of the specialised organisations or agencies to participate without vote in its deliberations and in those of the commissions established by it.

(3) The Economic and Social Council should adopt its own rules of procedure and the method of selecting its president.

CHAPTER X. SECRETARIAT

(1) There should be a secretariat comprising a secretary-general and such staff as may be required. The secretary-general should be the chief administrative officer of the organisation. He should be elected by the General Assembly on recommendation of the Security Council, for such term and under such conditions as are specified in the Charter.

(2) The secretary-general should act in that capacity in all meetings of the General Assembly, of the Security Council, and of the Economic and Social Council, and should make an annual report to the General Assembly on the work of the organisation.

(3) The secretary-general should have the right to bring to the attention of the Security Council any matter which in his opinion may threaten international peace and security.

CHAPTER XI. AMENDMENTS

Amendments should come into force for all members of the organisation when they have been adopted by a vote of two-thirds of the members of the General Assembly and ratified in accordance with their respective constitutional processes by the members of the organisation having permanent membership on the Security Council and by a majority of the other members of the organisation.

CHAPTER XII. TRANSITIONAL ARRANGEMENTS

(1) Pending the coming into force of the special agreement or agreements referred to in chapter VIII, section (B), paragraph (5), and in accordance

with the provisions of paragraph 5 of the Four-Nation Declaration, signed at Moscow on 30 October, 1943, the States parties to that declaration should consult with one another and as occasion arises with other members of the organisation with a view to such joint action on behalf of the organisation as may be necessary for the purpose of maintaining international peace and security.

(2) No provision of the charter should preclude action taken or authorised in relation to enemy States as a result of the present war by the governments having responsibility for such action.

Appendix 3

THE UNITING FOR PEACE RESOLUTION (377(V))

The General Assembly,

Recognising that the first two stated Purposes of the United Nations are:

'To maintain international peace and security, and to that end: to take effective collective measures for the prevention and removal of threats to the peace, and for the suppression of acts of aggression or other breaches of the peace, and to bring about by peaceful means, and in conformity with the principles of justice and international law, adjustment or settlement of international disputes or situations which might lead to a breach of the peace,' and

'To develop friendly relations among nations based on respect for the principle of equal rights and self-determination of peoples, and to take other appropriate measures to strengthen universal peace',

Reaffirming that it remains the primary duty of all members of the United Nations, when involved in an international dispute, to seek settlement of such a dispute by peaceful means through the procedures laid down in chapter VI of the charter, and recalling the successful achievements of the United Nations in this regard on a number of previous occasions,

Finding that international tension exists on a dangerous scale,

Recalling its resolution 290 (IV) entitled 'Essentials of peace', which states that disregard of the Principles of the charter of the United Nations is primarily responsible for the continuance of international resolution,

Reaffirming the importance of the exercise by the Security Council of its primary responsibility for the maintenance of international peace and security, and the duty of the permanent members to seek unanimity and to exercise restraint in the use of the veto,

Reaffirming that the initiative in negotiating the agreements for armed forces provided for in article 43 of the charter belongs to the Security Council, and desiring to ensure that, pending the conclusion of such agreements, the United Nations has at its disposal means for maintaining international peace and security,

Conscious that failure of the Security Council to discharge its responsibilities on behalf of all the member States, particularly those responsibilities referred to in the two preceding paragraphs, does not relieve member States of their obligations or the United Nations of its responsibility under the charter to maintain international peace and security,

Recognising in particular that such failure does not deprive the General Assembly of its rights or relieve it of its responsibilities under the charter in regard to the maintenance of international peace and security,

Recognising that discharge by the General Assembly of its responabilities in these respects calls for possibilities of observation which would ascertain the facts and expose aggressors; for the existence of armed forces which could be used collectively; and for the possibility of timely recommendation by the General Assembly to members of the United Nations for collective action which, to be effective, should be prompt,

A

1. *Resolves* that if the Security Council, because of lack of unanimity of the permanent members, fails to exercise its primary responsibility for the maintenance of international peace and security in any case where there appears to be a threat to the peace, breach of the peace, or act of aggression, the General Assembly shall consider the matter immediately with a view to making appropriate recommendations to members for collective measures, including in the case of a breach of the peace or act of aggression the use of armed force when necessary, to maintain or restore international peace and security. If not in session at the time, the General Assembly may meet in emergency special session within twenty-four hours of the request therefore. Such emergency special session shall be called if requested by the Security Council on the vote of any seven members, or by a majority of the members of the United Nations;

2. *Adopts* for this purpose the amendments to its rules of procedure set north in the annex to the present resolution;

B

3. *Establishes* a Peace Observation Commission which, for the calendar years 1951 and 1952, shall be composed of fourteen members, namely: China, Colombia, Czechoslovakia, France, India, Iraq, Israel, New Zealand, Pakistan, Sweden, the Union of Soviet Socialist Republics, the United Kingdom of Great Britain and Northern Ireland, the United States of America, and Uruguay, and which could observe and report on the situation in any area where there exists international tension the continuance of which is likely to endanger the maintenance of international peace and security. Upon the invitation or with the consent of the State into whose territory the Commission would go, the General Assembly, or the Interim Committee when the Assembly is not in session, may utilise the Commission if the Security Council is not exercising the functions assigned to it by the charter with respect to the matter in question. Decisions to utilise the Commission shall be made on the affirmative vote of two-thirds of the members present and voting. The Security Council may also utilise the Commission in accordance with its authority under the charter;

4. *Decides* that the Commission shall have authority in its discretion to appoint sub-commissions and to utilise the services of observers to assist it in the performance of its functions;

5. *Recommends* to all governments and authorities that they co-operate with the Commission and assist it in the performance of its functions;

6. *Requests* the Secretary-General to provide the necessary staff and facilities, utilising, where directed by the Commission, the United Nations Panel of Field Observers envisaged in General Assembly resolution 297 B (IV);

C

7. *Invites* each member of the United Nations to survey its resources in order to determine the nature and scope of the assistance it may be in a position to render in support of any recommendations of the Security Council or of the General Assembly for the restoration of international peace and security;

8. *Recommends* to the States members of the United Nations that each member maintain within its national armed forces elements so trained, organised and equipped that they could promptly be made available, in accordance with its constitutional processes, for service as a United Nations unit or units, upon recommendation by the Security Council or the General Assembly, without prejudice to the use of such elements in exercise of the right of individual or collective self-defence recognised in article 51 of the charter;

9. *Invites* the members of the United Nations to inform the Collective Measures Committee provided for in paragraph 11 as soon as possible of the measures taken in implementation of the preceding paragraph;

10. *Requests* the Secretary-General to appoint, with the approval of the Committee provided for in paragraph 11, a panel of military experts who could be made available, on request, to member States wishing to obtain technical advice regarding the organisation, training, and equipment for prompt service as United Nations units of the elements referred to in paragraph 8;

D

11. *Establishes* a Collective Measures Committee consisting of fourteen members, namely: Australia, Belgium, Brazil, Burma, Canada, Egypt, France, Mexico, Philippines, Turkey, the United Kingdom of Great Britain and Northern Ireland, the United States of America, Venezuela and Yugoslavia, and directs the Committee, in consultation with the Secretary-General and with such member States as the Committee finds appropriate, to study and make a report to the Security Council and the General Assembly, not later than 1 September 1951, on methods, including those in section C of the present resolution, which might be used to maintain and strengthen international peace and security in accordance with the Purposes and Principles of the charter, taking account of collective self-defence and regional arrangements (articles 51 and 52 of the charter);

12. *Recommends* to all member States that they co-operate with the Committee and assist it in the performance of its functions;

13. *Requests* the Secretary-General to furnish the staff and facilities necessary for the effective accomplishment of the purposes set forth in sections C and D of the present resolution;

E

14. *Is fully conscious* that, in adopting the proposals set forth above, enduring peace will not be secured solely by collective security arrangements against breaches of international peace and acts of aggression, but that a genuine and lasting peace depends also upon the observance of all the Principles and Purposes established in the charter of the United

Nations, upon the implementation of the resolutions of the Security Council, the General Assembly and other principal organs of the United Nations intended to achieve the maintenance of international peace and security, and especially upon respect for and observance of human rights and fundamental freedoms for all and on the establishment and maintenance of conditions of economic and social well-being in all countries; and accordingly

15. *Urges* member States to respect fully, and to intensify, joint action, in co-operation with the United Nations, to develop and stimulate universal respect for and observance of human rights and fundamental freedoms, and to intensify individual and collective efforts to achieve conditions of economic stability and social progress, particularly through the development of under-developed countries and areas.

302nd plenary meeting
3 November 1950

Appendix 4

RESOLUTION 1541 (XV)

Principles which should guide members in determining whether or not an obligation exists to transmit the information called for under article 73 (e) of the charter

The General Assembly,

Considering the objectives set forth in chapter XI of the charter of the United Nations,

Bearing in mind the list of factors annexed to General Assembly resolution 742 (VIII) of 27 November 1953,

Having examined the report of the Special Committee of Six on the Transmission of Information under Article 73 (e) of the Charter, appointed under General Assembly resolution 1467 (XIV) of 12 December 1959 to study the principles which should guide members in determining whether or not an obligation exists to transmit the information called for in article 73 (e) of the charter and to report on the results of its study to the Assembly at its fifteenth session,

1. *Expresses its appreciation* of the work of the Special Committee of Six on the Transmission of Information under Article 73 (e) of the Charter;

2. *Approves* the principles set out in section V, part B, of the report of the Committee, as amended and as they appear in the annex to the present resolution;

3. *Decides* that these principles should be applied in the light of the facts and the circumstances of each case to determine whether or not an obligation exists to transmit information under article 73 (e) of the charter.

948th plenary meeting
15 December 1960

ANNEX

Principles which should guide members in determining whether or not an obligation exists to transmit the information called for in article 73 (e) of the charter of the United Nations

Principle I

The authors of the charter of the United Nations had in mind that chapter XI should be applicable to territories which were then known to be of the colonial type. An obligation exists to transmit information under article 73 (e) of the charter in respect of such territories whose peoples have not yet attained a full measure of self-government.

APPENDIX 4

Principle II

Chapter XI of the charter embodies the concept of non-self-governing territories in a dynamic state of evolution and progress towards a 'full measure of self-government'. As soon as a territory and its peoples attain a full measure of self-government, the obligation ceases. Until this comes about, the obligation to transmit information under article 73 (e) continues.

Principle III

The obligation to transmit information under article 73 (e) of the charter constitutes an international obligation and should be carried out with due regard to the fulfilment of international law.

Principle IV

Prima facie there is an obligation to transmit information in respect of a territory which is geographically separate and is distinct ethnically and/or culturally from the country administering it.

Principle V

Once it has been established that such a *prima facie* case of geographical and ethnical or cultural distinctness of a territory exists, other elements may then be brought into consideration. These additional elements may be, *inter alia*, of an administrative, political, juridical, economic or historical nature. If they affect the relationship between the metropolitan State and the territory concerned in a manner which arbitrarily places the latter in a position or status of subordination, they support the presumption that there is an obligation to transmit information under article 73 (e) of the charter.

Principle VI

A non-self-governing territory can be said to have reached a full measure of self-government by:
(*a*) Emergence as a sovereign independent State;
(*b*) Free association with an independent State; or
(*c*) Integration with an independent State.

Principle VII

(*a*) Free association should be the result of a free and voluntary choice by the peoples of the territory concerned expressed through informed and democratic processes. It should be one which respects the individuality and the cultural characteristics of the territory and its peoples, and retains for the peoples of the territory which is associated with an independent State the freedom to modify the status of that territory through the expression of their will by democratic means and through constitutional processes.

(*b*) The associated territory should have the right to determine its internal constitution without outside interference, in accordance with due constitutional processes and the freely expressed wishes of the people. This does not preclude consultations as appropriate or necessary under the terms of the free association agreed upon.

Principle VIII

Integration with an independent State should be on the basis of complete equality between the peoples of the erstwhile non-self-governing territory and those of the independent country with which it is integrated. The peoples of both territories should have equal status and rights of citizenship and equal guarantees of fundamental rights and freedoms without any distinction or discrimination; both should have equal rights and opportunities for representation and effective participation at all levels in the executive, legislative and judicial organs of government.

Principle IX

Integration should have come about in the following circumstances:

(a) The integrating territory should have attained an advanced stage of self-government with free political institutions, so that its peoples would have the capacity to make a responsible choice through informed and democratic processes;

(b) The integration should be the result of the freely expressed wishes of the territory's peoples acting with full knowledge of the change in their status, their wishes having been expressed through informed and democratic processes, impartially conducted and based on universal adult suffrage. The United Nations could, when it deems it necessary, supervise these processes.

Principle X

The transmission of information in respect of non-self-governing territories under article 73 (e) of the charter is subject to such limitation as security and constitutional considerations may require. This means that the extent of the information may be limited in certain circumstances, but the limitation in article 73 (e) cannot relieve a member State of the obligations of chapter XI. The 'limitation' can relate only to the quantum of information of economic, social and educational nature to be transmitted.

Principle XI

The only constitutional considerations to which article 73 (e) of the charter refers are those arising from constitutional relations of the territory with the administering member. They refer to a situation in which the constitution of the territory gives it self-government in economic, social and educational matters through freely elected institutions. Nevertheless, the responsibility for transmitting information under article 73 (e) continues, unless these constitutional relations preclude the government or parliament of the administering member from receiving statistical and other information of a technical nature relating to economic, social and educational conditions in the territory.

Principle XII

Security considerations have not been invoked in the past. Only in very exceptional circumstances can information on economic, social and educational conditions have any security aspect. In other circumstances, therefore, there should be no necessity to limit the transmission of information on security grounds.

106

Appendix 5

RESOLUTION 1514 (XV)

Declaration on the granting of independence to colonial countries and peoples

The General Assembly,

Mindful of the determination proclaimed by the peoples of the world in the charter of the United Nations to reaffirm faith in fundamental human rights, in the dignity and worth of the human person, in the equal rights of men and women and of nations large and small and to promote social progress and better standards of life in larger freedom,

Conscious of the need for the creation of conditions of stability and well-being and peaceful and friendly relations based on respect for the principles of equal rights and self-determination of all peoples, and of universal respect for, and observance of, human rights and fundamental freedoms for all without distinction as to race, sex, language or religion,

Recognising the passionate yearning for freedom in all dependent peoples and the decisive role of such peoples in the attainment of their independence,

Aware of the increasing conflicts resulting from the denial of or impediments in the way of the freedom of such peoples, which constitute a serious threat to world peace,

Considering the important role of the United Nations in assisting the movement for independence in trust and non-self-governing territories,

Recognising that the peoples of the world ardently desire the end of colonialism in all its manifestations,

Convinced that the continued existence of colonialism prevents the development of international economic co-operation, impedes the social, cultural and economic development of dependent peoples and militates against the United Nations' ideal of universal peace,

Affirming that peoples may, for their own ends, freely dispose of their natural wealth and resources without prejudice to any obligations arising out of international economic co-operation, based upon the principle of mutual benefit, and international law,

Believing that the process of liberation is irresistible and irreversible and that, in order to avoid serious crises, an end must be put to colonialism and all practices of segregation and discrimination associated therewith,

Welcoming the emergence in recent years of a large number of dependent territories into freedom and independence, and recognising the increasingly powerful trends towards freedom in such territories which have not yet attained independence,

Convinced that all peoples have an inalienable right to complete freedom, the exercise of their sovereignty and the integrity of their national territory,

Solemnly proclaims the necessity of bringing to a speedy and unconditional end colonialism in all its forms and manifestations;

And to this end

Declares that:

1. The subjection of peoples to alien subjugation, domination and exploitation constitutes a denial of fundamental human rights, is contrary to the charter of the United Nations and is an impediment to the promotion of world peace and co-operation.

2. All peoples have the right to self-determination; by virtue of that right they freely determine their political status and freely pursue their economic, social and cultural development.

3. Inadequacy of political, economic, social or educational preparedness should never serve as a pretext for delaying independence.

4. All armed action or repressive measures of all kinds directed against dependent peoples shall cease in order to enable them to exercise peacefully and freely their right to complete independence, and the integrity of their national territory shall be respected.

5. Immediate steps shall be taken, in trust and non-self-governing territories or all other territories which have not yet attained independence, to transfer all powers to the peoples of those territories, without any conditions or reservations, in accordance with their freely expressed will and desire, without any distinction as to race, creed or colour, in order to enable them to enjoy complete independence and freedom.

6. Any attempt aimed at the partial or total disruption of the national unity and the territorial integrity of a country is incompatible with the purposes and principles of the charter of the United Nations.

7. All States shall observe faithfully and strictly the provisions of the charter of the United Nations, the Universal Declaration of Human Rights, and the present declaration on the basis of equality, non-interference in the internal affairs of all States, and respect for the sovereign rights of all peoples and their territorial integrity.

947th plenary meeting
14 December 1960

INDEX

Aggression, 2, 28
Anguilla, 69

Bank for International Settlements, 74

Certain Expenses of the United Nations
case, 6, 8, 22–4, 38–40
China, 3
civil war, 35, 37
Collective Measures Committee, 20,
24
colonialism, 4–5, 61–2
conference for reviewing Charter, 9, 10
Congo, 33–6
Cook Islands, 65
Cyprus, 40

Declaration on Granting of Independence—Resolution 1514 (XV), 50,
58, 60–3, App. 5
declaratory resolutions, 62–3
Dumbarton Oaks proposals, 14–16,
17, 25, 28, 48, 72, App. 2

Economic and Social Council:
composition and functions, 72, 73
increase in membership, 10–11
enforcement action, 16–17, 23, 24, 25,
29, 37, 39
European Economic Community, 74
European Free Trade Association, 74

factors indicating attainment of self-
government, etc., 55–7
First Admissions case, 5
free association, 59

General Agreement on Trade and
Tariffs, 74
General Assembly:
responsibility for economic matters,
73
responsibility for maintenance of
peace and security, 38–9, 43
Gibraltar, 66, 67

Human rights, international covenants,
53, 70, 71

independence, 3, 49, 50, 51, 66
Injuries case, 5, 6
International Bank, 74
International Monetary Fund, 74
International trade, promotion of, 5

Katanga, attempted secession, 33–4
Korea, 6, 19, 29

Law:
of international trade, definition, 84
of the United Nations, development
of, 5, 7–8
League of Nations: 4, 7, 14–15, 48
Council, powers of, 15
Covenant, defects in, 14–15

mandated territories, 48
mercenaries in Congo, 35–6, 37
Military Staff Committee, 18, 25

non-self-governing territories:
resolutions concerning, 57, 59
implementation of declaration, 62–5
nuclear weapons, 2

ONUC, 22, 33–5:
legal basis, 37–8
Organisation for European Co-operation and Development, 74
outer space, 2, 63

peace-keeping operations 23, 28–42,
44
Peace-keeping Operations Committee,
43–4
Peace Observation Committee, 20
police action, 6, 29–31
Principles regarding Article 73 (e) of
the Charter, 58–60

Rhodesia, 12, 64

San Francisco conference, 2, 4, 21, 28, 48, 51, 52, 53, 68, 72, 85
Secretary-General:
  functions in respect of ONUC, 33, 34
  functions in respect of UNCITRAL, 81
  functions in respect of UNIDO, 79
Security Council:
  action in respect of Korea, 29, 30
  enforcement powers, 4
  genesis in Dumbarton Oaks proposals, 16
  increase in membership, 10–11
  lack of unanimity of permanent members, 3, 20–1, 31
  mandatory decisions reserved for, 26
  number of non-permanent members, 10–11
  primary responsibility for maintenance of peace, 25, 38–9
  voting formula, 18–19
  voting procedure, 19
self-determination, 50, 51, 52, 56, 65:
  characterisation of, 62
  recent views on scope of, 66–9
South West Africa, 12
special agreements (Article 43), 17, 18
Special Committee on Colonialism, 63–4
Special Committee on Friendly Relations, 7–8, 67
specialised agencies, 74, 81
States:
  developed and developing, 5, 79
  emergence of, 3, 4–5

trusteeship system, 48–9

UNCITRAL, 80–4:
  discussions in General Assembly, 80
  first session, 84
  constitutional basis, 85
UNCTAD, 75–80:
  conferences, 75
  constitutional basis, 77–8
  Trade and Development Board, 79
UNEF, 22–3, 31–3:
  legal basis, 36
  withdrawal, 45
UNFICYP, 40–1:
  legal basis, 41–2
UNIDO, 75, 78–9:
  constitutional basis, 79–80
  Industrial Development Board, 79
UNIDROIT, 81, 82, 84
United Nations:
  capacity for development, 8
  Charter—amendment procedure, 9–11
  forces, 4, 29
  present membership, 2
  Purposes and Principles, 1, 8, 25, 37, 51, 63, 77, App. 1
Uniting for Peace resolution, 6, 7, 19, 20, 32, 34:
  conformity with Charter, 20–2
UNTEA, 42:
  legal basis, 42–3

veto, 24, 26
visiting missions, 60

UNITED NATIONS CHARTER

Article 1: 54, 77, 78
Article 1 (1): 25, 29, 37, 42
Article 1 (2): 52, 68, 70
Article 1 (3): 78, 75
Article 2 (4): 8, 15, 67
Article 2 (7): 37
Article 3: 85
Article 7: 73
Article 10: 23, 25
Article 11 (1): 27
Article 11 (2): 21, 22–3, 24, 25, 27
Article 12: 22, 25
Article 13: 77, 78
Article 14: 23, 25
Article 17 (2): 22, 38
Article 22: 77, 78, 79

Article 23: 10–11
Article 27: 10–11
Article 35: 22, 23
Article 36 (1): 42
Article 39: 30
Article 40: 37
Article 42: 18, 30
Article 43: 16, 18, 27, 29, 30
Article 51: 20, 26
Article 52 (3): 19
Article 55: 54, 78
Article 55 (b): 78
Article 55 (c): 65
Article 57: 74
Article 60: 78
Article 61: 10

INDEX

Article 63: 74
Article 68: 75, 78
Article 73: 50, 53, 59, 61, 62
Article 73 (e): 54, 55, 56, 59, 65

Article 76: 53
Article 108: 9, 10, 13
Article 109: 9, 10, 13

GENERAL ASSEMBLY RESOLUTIONS REFERRED TO IN THE TEXT

66 (I)	1000 (ES I)	1752 (XVII)
219 (III)	1001 (ES I)	1756 (XVII)
267 (III)	1136 (XII)	1815 (XVII)
332 (IV)	1381 (XIV)	1991 (XVIII)
334 (IV)	1467 (XIV)	2089 (XX)
567 (VI)	1514 (XV)	2102 (XX)
648 (VII)	1541 (XV)	2152 (XXI)
742 (VIII)	1654 (XVI)	2189 (XXI)
992 (X)	1670 (XVI)	2205 (XXI)
997 (ES I)	1707 (XVI)	2206 (XXI)
998 (ES I)	1731 (XVI)